Discovering Edith Stein
in a
Daisy Wreath of Friends

Edith Stein

Discovering Edith Stein in a Daisy Wreath of Friends

Pat Lyne, OCDS

To the 'Nottey' family — at large!
With my love.
Pat
12/8/04.

GRACEWING

First published in 2004

Gracewing
2 Southern Avenue, Leominster
Herefordshire HR6 0QF

ISBN 0 85244 631 4

Typeset by Action Publishing Technology Ltd,
Gloucester GL1 5SR

Printed in England by
Antony Rowe Ltd, Eastbourne BN23 6QT

Contents

List of Illustrations

Introduction

A discerning reviewer of *Edith Stein Discovered* wrote: 'I suspect that Pat Lyne's own journey as a member of the Secular Order of Carmel is somehow caught up with Edith Stein.' This book is intended as a sequel to *Edith Stein Discovered* and is inevitably a personal memoir, as true as possible. At times it is a painful reliving of the past but it also opens further windows on Edith's life and work. I draw portraits of those who have assisted my journey with grateful thanks. Friends may come and go but those who endure are purest gold. Edith is one who endures.

On 3 August 1916 Edith Stein was awarded her doctorate *summa cum laude*. The few friends who celebrated with Edith on that day crowned her with a wreath woven with ivy and daisies. After the party she walked home, wearing the wreath, and was greeted by her landlady: 'One ought to take your picture like that, while the glow of happiness is still there. Otherwise, you've always got such a serious look on your face.' It is good to have this happy memory of someone who is so often seen to be a tragic figure.

Circumstance and people, a daisy chain of events, have guided my journey of 'Discovering Edith'. In view of the quotation above, it has become a daisy wreath. As I grow older and life becomes more and more solitary, I continue to value Edith as a daily companion. I would like to think others might do so, after sharing my journey.

Pat Lyne, OCDS
9 August 2003

CHAPTER ONE

A Prologue

In a hidden corner of the Welsh Border town of Presteigne lies a small, private cemetery in which there are sixteen graves. Fourteen of them are Carmelite sisters. I was at the graveside for the burial of eleven but not for the one who provides the starting point for this story.

Charlotte Spitz was born in Berlin on 25 June 1893. Her parents were Jewish and her father a successful banker. The death of a sister (three years older than herself) had a profound effect on nine-year-old 'Lotte'. As a youngster she was musically very gifted and had dreams of becoming a great singer. Her health was poor and, guided by her parents, she decided on an academic career and went to university in 1912 where she studied science and modern languages. When war broke out, she worked as a volunteer nurse from August 1914 until November 1915. Following this, she resumed her university studies, broadening her interests by attending lectures on music, literature, philosophy and psychology, ultimately obtaining a Ph.D. in the history of music.

She was subsequently bedridden for many months with TB of the spine, during which time she was music critic for several Berlin journals, typing her articles while lying flat on her back. She lost both her parents in the mid-thirties and on a visit to relatives in England she met Father Vincent McNabb under whose influence she converted to Christianity. She was received into the Catholic Church in 1936. She did not return to Germany and little is known about her life in these years.

A note tells me that she attended a music festival in Cambridge as a correspondent for a German journal in 1938.

Her Christian faith played a significant role in her life, and as a Dominican Tertiary she lived simply, caring for the down-and-outs at St Joseph's, Malden Road. The life of a German Jew during the war years in England was far from easy and prayer became more and more a way of life for Lotte. In 1945 – she would have been fifty-two-years-old by then – she accompanied a friend on a visit to the Carmel of Berkhamstead in Hertfordshire. She immediately felt at home and a strong call to Carmel, and shortly afterwards asked to be received into the community. In January 1946 she was given the habit and the name of Sister Magdalen of Jesus and she made her profession the following year.

The community she joined had a charismatic prioress, Mother Michael of the Holy Trinity. The sisters were very 'earthbound' and earned their living from their livestock, mostly sheep, goats and hens. They were keen gardeners and believed in self-sufficiency. This was not an easy environment for Lotte. She was after all an academic, not very strong physically and already way past mid-life. She was ill-equipped for the strenuous work of tending livestock and the everyday domestic tasks of Carmelite life. At different times she was asked to act as provisor, linen officer, and sacristan, this last task being very close to her heart. A member of her community remembers her as tall and of striking appearance, as a deeply spiritual person given to prayer and of a very high intellectual order. Whenever she chanted the psalms in Hebrew for her sisters it opened another world and the comment in her obituary – 'she could have taught us so much' – suggests a sadness that time was not allowed for this.

In 1950 Mother Michael was invited by Bishop Petit of Menevia to bring her community to Wales. Being – I believe – a pioneer at heart, she bravely accepted the challenge. In 1951 she took her fourteen sisters to Presteigne where a Grade II listed house, in poor condition after wartime occupation by the army, had been purchased. Greenfields had four acres, a cow shed, a walled garden and greenhouse and a stable block. Mother Michael could see potential in such a place and surely her pioneering spirit overtook her undoubted wisdom.

Sister Magdalen and a small group of young sisters were the

advance party and had the task of preparing the house for the remainder. On each occasion the sisters travelled in cattle trucks alongside their precious livestock. The first contingent consisted of sheep and goats, the second of hens and the pony, Marjorie. All too soon it must have been apparent how inadequate the house was for a community of Carmelite sisters. There were insufficient rooms, and wooden huts were erected on the lawn in which many of them slept for nine years. They could not afford builders, and at Mother Michael's bidding the sisters set to as carpenters and bricklayers, firstly transforming the conservatory into a temporary public chapel. In 1953 an annexe was built and, as the sisters' skills increased, they worked away on the building of their own chapel, the conversion of the stable block as extern living quarters, and a quadrangle of cells and offices which were created from railway sleepers. This work was finally completed by 1960. Meanwhile, the ceremony of enclosure had taken place in 1956. The chapel foundation stone was laid in 1954 but the consecration did not take place until 1976. There is little doubt that the health of many sisters suffered later as a result of the quite extraordinary hardships they endured.

It is not too surprising that by 1959 Sister Magdalen's health failed her. She had become very frail physically with severe curvature of the spine and was eventually confined to a wheelchair. Her physical suffering seemed to draw her closer in spirit to the suffering of her fellow Jews in Europe. She was only sixty-six but her heart was worn out and she died peacefully in May 1960. She was the second sister to be buried in the little cemetery, where this story begins. Sister Marylis had predeceased her in 1953 and was the first sister laid to rest in the Carmelite graveyard.

I discovered a strong thread of sameness in the lives of Charlotte Spitz and Edith Stein. Lotte was born a mere two years later than Edith, of Jewish parents. She too was full of childish dreams of achieving something great, she too was an academic who attended university, who nursed during the First World War, who converted to Christianity and who became a Carmelite: a carbon copy, you might think, of Edith's life. They parted company only when Charlotte travelled to England and Edith to Auschwitz.

I have no means of knowing how close a relationship

Charlotte engaged in with Edith's life but we can safely assume that she felt a sisterly closeness to one whose pilgrimage was so similar to her own. The Presteigne community were aware that the suffering of her nation was never far from her thoughts or her prayers. There is little doubt that in this time she acquired a devotion to Edith which she shared with her community. On feast days she prepared prayer cards for her sisters with a quotation from Edith Stein's writings carefully typed on the back. Was she, I wonder, in touch with Edith's community of Cologne who, after the war, returned to their original home in the Schnurgasse? Their monastery had been severely bomb-damaged and they prepared to rebuild and restore it with their own hands. Was Mother Michael taking inspiration and encouragement from their enterprise? It seems a remarkable coincidence that unskilled women should undertake such a task – and succeed both in Germany and in Wales – in the post-war years.

Sister Magdalen Spitz died in 1960. She left her love of Edith Stein with her community and twenty-five years later, I too inherited that love. I have to try to explain how this came about.

* * * * *

A small memento of Sister Magdalen's devotion to Edith Stein was found recently by a member of her community. Written in the 1950s, before the cause for Edith's beatification had been opened, it is typewritten on a small square of cream paper and pasted onto a slightly larger piece of blue card. There is a pinhole in this which indicates that it was attached to a noticeboard where others would notice it and pray with her. The title is in red print and space ran out before 'Stein' was completed.

> Prayer for the Beatification of
> Sr Teresia Benedicta of the Cross, E. St
>
> O God, Thou eternal Being and origin
> of all things, we thank Thee for the
> great gifts and graces which Thou hast
> bestowed on Thy servant Teresia Bene-
> dicta of the Cross to present her to

us as a light of knowledge and an example of all virtues. We beseech Thine infinite Majesty: glorify Thy servant and let her share in the honour of the altars, as she sought nothing on earth but through the Cross of Thy Son to save souls and to glorify Thy Name. Who livest and reignest for ever and ever. Amen.

(Copied from the original)

CHAPTER TWO

A New Life at Fifty-Five

In the 1970s I was living in Herefordshire with a friend. She was a nurse and I ran a small thirty-five-acre farm - Redgates - and Connemara pony stud. We attended the nearest Catholic church where the parish priest was a Benedictine monk of Belmont. It was a rural area and we found it a sharp contrast to the busy parish life in Aylesbury, Buckinghamshire from where we had come.

We were both very committed to the pony breeding. This involved hard work and dedication but was repaid in the quality of the ponies we bred and the success we achieved with them. Life was full and we made many new friends. The only downside was Jo's indifferent health. My diary reminds me how often we visited hospital for X-rays and consultant appointments and it seemed to have no end.

During my years in Aylesbury I had been an enthusiastic member of the Legion of Mary. The apostolic work was challenging and my 'patch' included the spinal unit at Stoke Mandeville hospital, the psychiatric prison at Grendon Underwood and Katie, a nine-year-old with leukaemia. I remember so well my home visits to prepare Katie for her First Holy Communion. In spite of being confined to her bedroom and having to wear a wig Katie remained a dear, happy little girl. We were able to see her pony from the window and dream together about the day she would ride him again. Our shared love of ponies made my heart-rending task a little easier than it might otherwise have been. Katie made her First Holy

Communion in her bedroom, with only her mother, Father Galvin and myself present. She died a few weeks later, long before medicine had found a way of dealing with childhood leukaemia.

As President of the Aylesbury Praesidium and of the Curia I was rarely at home in the evenings. My holidays were spent on Peregrinatio Pro Christo which took me to a slum parish in Philadelphia, to Russia for three weeks and as an envoy to Iceland. No wonder I was a lost soul without the Legion and the many riches it brought to my life. It left a gap waiting to be filled.

In the spring of 1971 Jo was on night duty in the County Hospital. One evening she noticed a nun sitting beside a patient's bed. She later discovered the nun and the patient were Carmelite sisters; both of them were happy to find a Catholic nurse in charge. They soon became friends. When Sister Teresa returned home, Jo received an open invitation to visit the Carmelite monastery at Presteigne. Sister Teresa died in August 1971 and hers was the third grave in the Carmelite cemetery.

I well remember the dull October day on which I drove Jo to Presteigne for a weekend retreat. I found the grey stone building and entrance to the 'turn' cold and forbidding and wondered how she would find the solace she was seeking in such a place. On my return three days later, she was aglow with happiness. I was taken to see the chapel and shared Vespers with her and the sisters for the first time. My memory falters as I try to recall how our friendship with the community developed. There was an invitation to a Silver Jubilee celebration Mass and then a funeral for the same sister, which took place in 1979. Meanwhile Sister Catherine – or Mother Catherine as she was better known – had been buried in 1975. She was a redoubtable lady who entered Carmel at the ripe age of fifty-six, who died in her eighty-sixth year on the twenty-ninth anniversary of her profession and who had served the community as both prioress and novice mistress. Thus crosses were erected on the fourth and fifth graves in the Carmelite cemetery.

As time passed, I was occasionally asked to drive the sisters to various appointments. In 1976 I realized they had a serious problem when Sister Flora was no longer able to manage their livestock and the four acres on which they grazed. I offered to arrange the sale of the cattle and undertook the care of the land. This entailed regular visits to Presteigne – some fifteen miles distant – and I invariably arranged them to coincide with Mass or Vespers. I was very drawn to the aura of prayer and peace that I experienced on these visits. The simplicity of the chapel and the kindness of the sisters, when I met them in the parlour, were an added attraction. Slowly but surely I discovered the gap in my life was being filled by Carmel, not in the way I might have anticipated or even hoped, but it provided me with a focus beyond my day-to-day duties at Redgates.

In time, it became obvious that I was seeking a deeper commitment, something beyond driving the car here and there, beyond the care of livestock. Did it lie in Carmel? If so, in what direction? In spite of Mother Catherine's admirable example of entering Carmel at the age I was about to reach, I did not believe I had such an absolute vocation. Perhaps joining the Third Order would be the answer? I knew I needed *to belong*, to have a 'rule of thumb' for my spiritual life. When I presented the idea to Sister Anne, the prioress, it was not immediately greeted with enthusiasm. However, a monthly day of retreat was arranged for me with the use of a caravan on the perimeter of enclosure. This provided the opportunity to pray and to read and to leave all my daily concerns behind me. I joined the sisters in chapel for the Divine Office and spent an hour with a member of the community. She was my guide, my formation mistress, on my journey. It was a period during which I acquired an appreciation of the Carmelite charism and the Teresian saints. Inevitably I discerned a marked contrast to the very active apostolate of a Legionary to which I was accustomed. Our Lady's place as Patron of both the Legion of Mary and of Carmel provided a strong bond between the two. As time passed, my desire for a tangible commitment to Carmel increased and I waited patiently for the next move.

In the 1970s the Third Order had barely emerged from a pre-Vatican II interpretation of the commitment and lifestyle of a secular Carmelite. I realize, with the benefit of hindsight, that this was the reason for Sister Anne's hesitation when I made my first enquiry. I discovered, some considerable time later, that it was a challenging moment to become involved with the Third Order. The rebirth or renewal continues to take place as I write and I am pleased to have played a very small part in it.

In 1983 I received an unexpected phone call from Carmel. Abbot John Roberts of Downside was visiting and would receive me for formation in the Third Order at Vespers the following day. It was a simple ceremony, for which Jo joined me, and afterwards we had a cup of tea with the abbot. As he was naturally a very shy man, it took a while for us to know him and to realize his true worth. He became a much loved and trusted friend.

In October of the same year, a conference was held for Third Order members at a retreat centre near Crewe and I was lucky enough to attend. The three days had a profound impact and there was no question of looking back from that time forward.

1983 had been a busy year with my car constantly on the road. Two sisters, living temporarily away from Carmel, were brought home. It was hoped the community could care for them now they had younger sisters trying their vocation. Sister Margaret was in Nazareth House, Wrexham and was bedridden. On her return she was nursed with devotion by her own community. She died in September 1983 and was buried in the sixth grave. Sister Magdalen was much further from home, in the care of the Augustinian sisters of Burgess Hill. Sad to say, she was unable to resettle in Carmel and returned to Burgess Hill where she, too, died in September. She was brought home for her funeral Mass and burial and the seventh grave was dug. By sharing the illness, death and long journeys with the sisters I became a closer and ever closer friend of their community.

Since 1978 I had been writing a book on the history of the Connemara pony breed. I had no qualifications as an author but a deep love of the pony and its native habitat. The research and writing was undertaken inbetween running the stud farm, editing the *Connemara Chronicle* and responding to Carmelite needs. It took me six years, and as I drew to the end of my task Sister Anne invited me to stay in the guesthouse at Carmel, so that Sister Clare could assist me with the final artwork. This was in March 1984. The Hermitage, a small guest wing, became my home for the best part of a week. It is not easy to describe how very much 'at home' I felt as I answered each call of the monastery bell and joined the community at the offices throughout the day. I had only to cross the cobbled yard to enter the chapel and the prayer was a welcome respite from the concentrated work on *Shrouded in Mist*. Sister Clare was a tower of strength and without her assistance I doubt I would ever have completed such a huge undertaking.

On my final day at Presteigne I was deeply hurt. The chaplain was asked to bless the community's newly built infirmary wing, 'Bethania'. Kate and Josie – who were attached to the monastery living outside the enclosure – served the community in a variety of ways as, indeed, did I. They were invited to the ceremony. I was not. In the evening I was asked to the parlour and was offered an apology. The conversation moved on and Sister Anne expressed concern over the unsuitable help they had in the guesthouse. Might I consider taking on the job? In the past I had occasionally expressed the possibility of such an idea but without giving it any very serious thought. But, on that fateful evening of 16 March, I suddenly found myself saying 'Yes'. Surely the hand of God was on my shoulder as I did so. Looking back, nearly twenty years later, I realize that I saw a need and with God's grace I responded to it. In my work as a Legionary this had become second nature, responding to needs. On this occasion, the need had far deeper implications and the following morning I wondered if I would have the courage to see it through.

Redgates would have to be sold, my partnership with Jo broken, all my stock except for two ponies and a few sheep dispersed. It was a monumental undertaking. Sister Anne gave me a holy picture on the reverse of which she wrote, 'Thank you Pat for giving yourself to us and to Him all in one breath, the eve of St Patrick, March 16th 1984.' I had to keep this dual 'purpose' constantly in my heart and my sight as I began each new day throughout the following difficult six months.

Rather to my surprise, family and friends were very understanding when I told them my plans for the future. Even Jo, whom it would affect directly, was generous enough to realize it was something I felt called to do. I was, however, a little shaken when Abbot John did not entirely approve of my decision. He gave the impression he would have advised caution had I asked his advice. He, better than most, was aware of all the difficulties 'enclosure' presents and realized I might not find it easy. His letter in reply to mine concluded, 'Good luck anyhow'; so typical of dear Father John.

1984 was an extraordinary year both for the community and for myself. As one emergency after another arose, I realized how right it was that I should be planning to live at Carmel and be available to them at all times. In April I was asked to drive to Darlington to bring Mother Michael 'home'. She had spent the last four years as a member of Darlington Carmel but after suffering a small stroke she realized death was not far off. She asked to return to the Carmel she had established thirty-five years earlier. I found the journey long and stressful with a sick, frail old sister sitting motionless on the rear seat with the infirmarian clasping her hand. Mother Michael died at peace a few days later. Her funeral Mass was celebrated on Easter Tuesday, in glorious sunshine, and she was laid to rest in the eighth grave.

In June, the community suffered the unexpected and tragic death of one of their younger sisters. It cast a huge cloud over the monastery and I sometimes wonder if it has ever lifted. I remember we were haymaking. Kate, Josie and I spent the afternoon turning the sweet, newly-mown grass row by row with wooden hay rakes. The sun was warm on our backs and we did not speak. How could the sun shine when there was sadness all around us? The ninth grave was dug.

The story of death seemed to haunt us, and in July dear Sister Francis died unexpectedly. For some months I had driven her to hospital, and back home again two or three days later, at regular intervals. She was suffering from anaemia and constant blood transfusions were necessary. She knew she was not going to make old age but sudden death in her early sixties was not anticipated. Three deaths in such a short space of time took its toll of the community. The tenth cross was erected in the cemetery.

Meanwhile I continued with the painful task of placing Redgates on the market, finding homes for the majority of the stock and, most importantly, looking for somewhere in Kington for Jo to live. Abbot John, wise man that he was, advised me to invest some of the proceeds from the sale of Redgates in a small property near the Carmel. He realized, even if I did not, that I would require 'a bolt hole' from time to time. A small red-brick cottage with two acres of land two miles down the road from the Carmel came on the market in June. It was as if it had dropped out of the sky as a special gift to me in my hour of need. What an important piece, in the jigsaw of my future, Combe Cottage has been.

In August I went to Ireland with a car full of books. The long-awaited moment for the launch of *Shrouded in Mist* had arrived. I had not envisaged the many difficulties publishing and distributing my own work might incur. I was so inspired by my subject that it seemed worthwhile to make the effort and to take the risks. I regularly pushed the reality of a printer's bill to the very back of my mind. Sales in Dublin were practically non-existent but once I reached County Galway and the West, the book received a warm welcome. As I sat beside the commentators' box on Clifden show day, signing book after book for pony friends, my cup was full and Carmel seemed a million miles away.

I returned to Redgates and the final packing up. Jo had arranged the tenancy of Parlours Bank, a delightful old-world cottage on the Hergest estate. She was taking the older of the two dogs, Tansy, and I the younger, Chloe. Jo's favourite pony, Chiltern Dragonfly, was registered in her name and a friend a mile up the road offered to care for her. My foundation mare, Arctic Moon, now aged twenty-four and her fourteen-year-old daughter, Chiltern Gazelle, together with six breeding ewes went with me to Presteigne. Our Jersey house cow, Celandine, and her companion, Gene, had been taken to the local abattoir amidst great sadness. All the remaining stock had been sold or found suitable homes. The house and yard were cleared and shipshape. I shut the wooden oak gates, made to our own design ten years earlier, for the last time on 25 September 1984.

* * * * *

The first four months at Carmel were a honeymoon period both for the community and myself. I was pleased to answer their every need and they were appreciative. I soon settled into a rhythm of prayer, joining the community at 7.00 a.m. for Lauds before feeding the livestock. Mass followed at 8.00 a.m. I rarely missed Vespers at 4.30 p.m. or Compline at 9.00 p.m.

The latter, I soon discovered, was the perfect way in which to end a day, whether it had been a good or a difficult one.

The role of guest mistress did not come easily to me. Domestic work had always been anathema, and cooking presented a problem. A dear friend, Penelope Betjeman, gave me a crash course. In a single day I learnt how to prepare five different dishes, from which my menu rarely strayed. I found making beds a very unappealing task. I so much preferred having a pitchfork in my hands, a bale of straw to break open and a stable to 'set fair'. This had, after all, been my early morning chore for the past forty years and it never failed to give me satisfaction.

There were no set working hours or regular off-duty ones and I was free to maintain much of my former life in-between attending to the sisters' needs. The two ponies produced foals and the sheep lambs. I accepted invitations to judge at horse shows but reduced my commitment to the Connemara Pony Society. I spent time with my family and friends though some of the latter drifted away. For the first time in my life I was subject to others. I had no responsibility, other than that of making visitors welcome. If there was a train to be met in the evening and a light supper to prepare for an incoming guest, I accepted the situation without question. I – and my car – were at the service of the community and I was content that this should be the case.

I retain a vivid memory of my first Christmas at Carmel. It was a happy time. I was awoken on Christmas morning by Carmelite carols, which the community sang beneath my bedroom window. After Mass they greeted me in the parlour with their homespun cards and gifts. I spent the day with my family. When I returned in the evening I found the sisters anxious for the oldest member of their community, eighty-eight-year-old Sister Kathleen.

Sister Kathleen and I had become friends some months earlier when she was unwell and required care at night. I undertook night duty once a week and felt privileged to be able to help in this way. My sole function was to remain awake, in case she awoke and required a drink or the commode. Occasionally she demanded – yes, she was a lady of character – an item that was not readily to hand. I was anxious not to venture beyond her cell, being very conscious of enclosure and the care I should take to observe it. My plea of 'Could you wait till morning?' was always firmly dismissed. To sit through the night in the simple railway sleeper-built cell with a low light and a peacefully sleeping old Carmelite sister was a memorable experience and remains with me to this day. Equally so does the invitation to join the community in prayer at her bedside as she slipped gently from this world to the next on St Stephen's night. The cross on Sister Kathleen's grave was the eleventh to be erected in the Presteigne cemetery.

The comparative ease with which I adapted to life at Carmel was interrupted in the New Year by a call to hospital for an operation on an old ankle injury. I was in hospital for less than a week but left it on crutches and in need of regular physiotherapy. During a month-long convalescence with my Augustinian friends at Boarbank Hall, I suffered post-op depression and frustration at being so long away from my new commitments. Shortly before I was due to return to Presteigne a dear friend, Sister Teresa of the Holy Child, became ill and died soon afterwards. She was a very warm person with whom I shared a love of nature and animals. We occasionally met for a chat in the parlour and her death was a personal loss. I was 'home' in time for her funeral Mass and the twelfth grave was prepared.

I returned to a changed situation in the extern quarters and for the first time experienced the difficulties of living beside enclosure. I found myself sharing the small extern cottage with two companions. They both worked within enclosure, baking altar bread and nursing. This in itself was divisive as I struggled to steer a happy ship on the 'outside'. We each had our own problems and were where we were, for very different reasons. We did not have a communal sitting room and rarely came together for meals. We lived our independent lives as we thought fit. Bathroom and kitchen were shared and we lived cheek by jowl in a very confined area. It was a far-from-ideal situation for any of us.

Communication between the community and myself was reduced to a minimum, visitors were scarce and many a time there was little for me to do. I felt isolated and unhappy and often crept down to Combe Cottage for the night. I suppose it was inevitable that I should begin to ask myself why I was where I was. I was fifty-five years old, had always been self-sufficient and my own boss. This was no longer the case and I was ill-prepared for the downside. I found I could not read, write or pray. I was experiencing 'the dark night of the soul' and was ill-equipped to deal with this new phenomenon.

Meanwhile, the community were experiencing their own problems. Not only had they endured six deaths in the recent past but their two novices, both strong-minded women in their thirties, were asked to leave when it was agreed they did not have a Carmelite vocation. Sadder still was the loss of another younger member of the community who suffered difficulties with her vocation shortly after celebrating her Silver Jubilee. She asked for a year's exclaustration and was never able to return to religious life. The loss of each one was a further 'death' and was felt deeply, both inside and outside enclosure.

In the meantime my own vocation as a member of the Third Order of Carmel continued under the guidance of Sister Mary Immaculata, more commonly and affectionately known as Paddy. We met once a fortnight. When I had completed the formation period I was ready to make my First Promise and did so during Vespers on 18 June 1985 with Abbot John presiding. I had taken one more rather shaky step on my Carmelite pilgrimage. A few rough edges had been knocked off a raw novice but there were many more to be removed.

I have never been good at sharing my innermost feelings but Jo was my closest confidante. Our friendship remained strong and we met often. I would occasionally open my heart to her but she maintained I should have realized that in my position at Carmel I was 'neither fish nor fowl'. I had chosen to be there. I must make the best of it. These were tough words but true. Because I was experiencing difficulty in 'finding God' in my current suffering, almost subconsciously, I was seeking a go-between. I found one in Edith Stein.

Enclosed with my 1985 Christmas card from the prioress was a poem, *Holy Night – In Remembrance of Christmas Eve 1936,* written by Edith Stein for her sister Rosa. It spoke to me in a very special way. I had travelled the same stony path as Rosa, while waiting patiently to become a Catholic thirty years earlier. The long wait was at my mother's request. Now it felt as if I was travelling another stony path. It would have been so easy to say, 'I have made a mistake, I am not doing this job very well – better to admit it and let the sisters find a more suitable person.' Instead I expressed an interest in Edith Stein and was lent a book from the monastery library, *Edith Stein* by Sister Teresia (Renata) de Spiritu Sancto (Posselt), OCD. It was covered in a worn dust-wrapper and provided my first photograph of Edith. She was in her Carmelite habit. The same photograph was included as a frontispiece and was the only one in the book. It was sufficient to stimulate my initial interest in this relatively unknown Carmelite.

Sister Renata writes in her 'Introduction', 'This account of Sister Teresia Benedicta is not meant to be a biography in the proper sense of the word, but is simply a series of recollections and testimonies, as faithful and exact as possible.' It was far more than this for me. How strange that I should immediately feel a strong affinity with this special woman, someone who was both a German and a Jew, and I in contrast a very traditional English woman. And yet I discovered our lives often ran on parallel lines and for this reason I found it easy to relate to her life and to become her friend.

As daughters of strong mothers, Edith and I shared the influence this had on us throughout our lives. In spite of this – or maybe because of this – Edith and I were both determined and ambitious as young women. We held fast to our convictions, and the Catholic faith (which came late to us both), once found, became the mainspring of our lives. We experienced similar difficulties in sharing our deepest emotions and were irresistibly drawn to Carmel. Neither of us was proficient with a sewing needle or a household broom – and this is where the comparisons end. My current sufferings were minuscule beside hers, my intellect a dwarf beside hers, my stamina and ability to pray a mere shadow of hers BUT I was certain I had found a friend; one in whom I could confide and who would understand my present difficulties. A light flickered at the end of my dark tunnel and I pursued it. Edith's life and character held an instant fascination for me. I was bent on 'discovering' the person 'masked' by the keen mind of the scholar, the tragic eyes and the rarely recognized gaiety of heart. In my quest I was once again able to pick up a book and to read with a purpose. I continued my Carmelite pilgrimage with Edith Stein at my side.

CHAPTER THREE

The First Daisies in the Wreath

A daisy wreath of friends and events encouraged and enhanced my friendship with Edith Stein. It was not 'by chance' that I was able to develop such a close relationship. As the petals of the daisies unfolded, and the stalks led me forward, my journey of 'discovery' unfolded step by step.

I and many others in the English-speaking world have good reason to be grateful to Donald Nicholl and Cecily Hastings for their translation of Renata Posselt's biography of Edith Stein. It was published by Sheed and Ward in 1952 and cost 15s. A second edition was published in the same year and indicates an immediate interest in the life of Edith Stein. The copy I have, and treasure, was a 1952 second edition.

Only very recently did I make contact with the first 'bud' in the daisy wreath, Donald Nicholl. Donald died in 1997 but I have had the pleasure of meeting his wife Dorothy and of reading the revised edition of his book *The Testing of Hearts*, and have thus gained an insight into this remarkable man. In the post-war years Donald was, Dorothy told me, a wandering scholar who included Germany in his travels. One day he found himself at the door of Cologne Carmel; he rang the bell and was invited to the parlour where he met Sister Renata. It was she who suggested he might translate her German biography of Edith Stein into English. On his return to England, in company with the linguist, Cecily Hastings, Donald undertook the task. There is little doubt that while doing so, he acquired both respect and affection for Edith.

The recurring link (or stalk) in the daisy wreath is an unlikely one: the meeting of the two 'C's in my life, Carmel and Connemara. As I spoke with Dorothy I learnt how she and Donald had often spent their summer holidays in Connemara, while their children were young. They came to love the area and on two occasions in his *Testing of Hearts* Donald draws a comparison between the Arab Christians of Bethlehem and the people of Connemara. Both left a similar impression on him, one of beauty, gentleness and kindness.

Donald wrote *The Testing of Hearts* (Donald Nicholl, *The Testing of Hearts: A Pilgrim's Journal*, DLT, London, 1998) mostly during the time he was Rector of the Ecumenical Institute for Theological Research (1981–1985) at Tantur, which is situated between Jerusalem and Bethlehem. Apart from my delight at our shared appreciation of Edith and Connemara, I was moved by two mental pictures that he shares with his readers.

Edith Stein was born on the Jewish Day of Atonement in 1891. This day, and indeed her Jewish heritage, were always important to Edith. Donald's experience of Yom Kippur in Jerusalem is emotive and I ask myself: did Edith come to mind as he observed the respect with which the Jews treated this significant day in their calendar? He writes: 'By the dawn of Yom Kippur all traffic within Jerusalem had stopped; Israeli radio and television had gone silent; the air itself was uncannily still that day . . . It was truly awesome – a touch of the eternal sabbath of God.'

During the war years of 1940–1945 I received my schooling from the Sacred Heart of Mary Sisters and it is they I have to thank for the gift of faith and my membership of the Catholic Church. Devotion to Our Lady was nurtured in those teenage years and later, when I was a member of the Legion of Mary, this devotion was 'lived' in a very positive way. Our Lady was special, our mother, the mother of Christ, goodness and holiness personified; but was she not a young Jewish girl who responded to all God asked of her and who stood at the foot of the Cross in obedience to him and love of her Son? So many paintings, icons and statues have her wreathed in haloes, stars and colourful robes. Why not love her and pray to her as she really was? This is a question I have often pondered. Donald Nicholl writes:

> I am led to tell you that what my sojourn in this land has changed as much as anything else is my image of Mary. In previous years, that could hardly have been any other than ... the image of some dreamy, ethereal young lady, untouched by everyday toil. But since that time I have met the peasant women of Galilee. So now the image that comes spontaneously to my mind is of a woman with strong hands, sinewy through much work; and of a face whose skin is rough from exposure to the sun and the wind; of feet that are broad-spread through climbing the hills around Nazareth barefoot; but above all, of eyes that are steady and a mouth that is firm through enduring the sorrows of the refugee, the poor and the oppressed.

Donald's portrait of Our Lady is very real and I value it. Of course I – like many another – have a small plaster statue of Mary from which I have not been parted in fifty years. And more recently an icon, *La Bruna*, of Our Lady of Mount Carmel hangs on my bedroom wall. It is the oldest image of our Blessed Mother used by the Carmelites and the 'style' is one of tenderness. It exudes warmth, love and peace.

In 1949 Donald wrote an article for the publication *Life of the Spirit*, a short quotation from which depicts his shrewd understanding and appreciation of Edith: 'for eleven years she was like an industrious bee collecting experience both of the world and of the Church, experience which included an intimate acquaintance with the foremost philosophers in Europe, a strong draught of worldly fame and, on the Church's side, a firm friendship both with the Benedictines at Beuron and the Dominican Sisters at St. Magdalena in Speyer. It was as if God had chosen her person for distilling all that is noblest in the world's history.'

The last section of Donald's book, *The Testing of Hearts*, has the title, *Testing unto Death* and is the journal he kept during the terminal months of his life when he knew he was dying. It is here that I found his final testimony to Edith Stein:

> This awareness of the spirit as triumphant in the face of death was enhanced for me when I translated the life of Edith Stein ... The book records the way in which she encouraged the other people who were in the train that was

taking them to Auschwitz, and has a lovely photograph of her. Looking out of the photograph is her face with these beautiful, beautiful eyes, as though they have seen further than almost any human being has seen. Often it's the eyes that count so much, a gaze: that's why I have around me now photographs of so many holy people who have accompanied me on my journey through life . . .

When I spoke to Dorothy, the same photograph of Edith was where Donald had left it, above his desk. I wish I had been lucky enough to meet and to know Donald Nicholl.

The Posselt biography lifted my reading 'block' and I became hungry for anything further in the written word concerning Edith Stein. I was lent another book from the monastery library, a second biography written nearly twenty years after the first. The writer, Waltraud Herbstrith, a Carmelite nun, Sister Teresia a Matre Dei, is a member of the Edith Stein Carmel, at Tübingen in Germany. This volume was translated into English from a fifth, expanded 1983 German edition in 1985. I was lent a first edition of the translation by Father Bernard Bonowitz, OCSO, published by Harper & Row. The jacket cover is a photograph of a glass window in the church of the Carmelites in Bonn-Pützchen. It depicts Edith wreathed in barbed wire and a Nazi guard with gun in his hand standing to her rear. It is too graphic for my taste. I found this book a very dense read in a close-set, small typeface and with the use of many quotations in an even smaller print. It demanded concentrated, careful reading.

Inevitably, Herbstrith bases her work essentially on the Posselt biography together with what had become available since its publication. This included Edith's autobiography and letters, and various spiritual writings. By this time, the Edith Stein archive in the Cologne Carmel had grown considerably and Herbstrith was also able to use material from there. This biography gave me access to valuable fresh insights into the person of Edith Stein.

Of particular interest to myself was her friendship with Professor Günther Schulemann, University Chaplain of Breslau and Vicar of the Cathedral. After her conversion, while on vacation in Breslau, Edith often visited the professor for tea, occasionally taking her sister Rosa with her. Their conversation was wide-ranging and examined present-day Judaism and the Jews' attitude to death. The latter was a taboo subject in Jewish circles. The professor, we are told, was aware that '[Edith] divided the day between prayer, study and an affectionate participation in the life of her family.' Occasionally the undercurrents in the Stein household required all Edith's sympathetic understanding, and the friendship of the professor must have been a welcome relief.

Maria Wilkens, a long-time President of the Association of German Catholic Women Teachers, expressed her admiration for Edith and her contribution to philosophy and wrote: 'It made me happy to see a woman of such intellectual prominence so deeply committed to the ideals of the Catholic women's movement.' In this paper *Erinnerungen an Edith Stein* (*Memories of Edith Stein*) (1962), she continues: 'Yet within her penetrating eyes lay something mysterious and solemn, and the contrast between this and her simplicity created a certain awe – at least in me.'

A fellow novice, Sister Electa, is quoted as saying, 'She had quite a lively temperament, and her passionate side sometimes showed itself in her beautiful, flashing eyes.' Yes. It was often the case that Edith's eyes made a deep impression on those whom she met.

A friend from her days in Göttingen writes, 'Being with her was always a blessing for me; I always came away a little bit richer – either my own thoughts grew clearer, or I came to see an old problem in a new light. She was especially good with children ... My son, born in 1923, was particularly dear to her. He came with me twice to Münster, and then once later on to Cologne, where he kissed her through the grille, even though he couldn't stand it.' Such comments immediately dispel the image of a stern intellectual or indeed of a distant, detached Carmelite. Edith was never afraid to show love for those around her.

Throughout her biography Herbstrith explores Edith's philosophy and her spirituality. She generously shares her appraisal with readers but inevitably they are personal to her. For myself who has little or no understanding of philosophy, her conjectures provided a helpful guide.

Herbstrith's publishers are incorrect to suggest (on the front and back flaps of the book jacket) that this was the *first* biography of Edith. And that the author 'knew her well'. It cannot be disputed that the Posselt is the first and seminal biography. Herbstrith was born in 1929 – the same year as myself – and was therefore only thirteen years old when Edith died in Auschwitz. These publisher's errors do not occur in the second edition and in any event do not take away from the valuable contribution her work has made towards a better knowledge and understanding of Edith Stein's life.

The second 'daisy bud' in the wreath of my journey is a Carmelite sister whose story adds a further touch of colour to the many pieces in my jigsaw of personalities. In 1949, Mechtild Wiedenhöver, a young German girl who was anxious to discern her vocation, found her way to the door of the Cologne Carmel where she was invited to meet Sister Renata. She tells me it was not Edith who drew her to Cologne – although she had read about her – it was, quite simply, the only Carmel to which she knew her way. During her conversation with Sister Renata they spoke of Edith, and Mechtild was aware of her photograph hanging on the wall in the sister's office. She spoke warmly of Edith, saying, 'She truly was a chosen soul.' During this visit Sister Renata took Mechtild for a walk in the monastery garden just as she had done with Donald Nicholl before her.

Mechtild was suffering from curvature of the spine and for this reason Sister Renata felt unable to accept her. The community were determined to restore the war damage to their cloister and church with their own hands, not having the money to pay builders to do the work. Only those in good health, able to undertake manual labour, were considered as postulants in the post-war years. Sister Renata recommended Mechtild to the Darlington Carmel in England. I assume she spoke good English. She was professed at Darlington on 16 January 1952 and took the religious name, Lucia of the Incarnation. Sister Renata continued to correspond with Sister Lucia until her own death in 1961. All German publications concerning Edith were automatically sent to Darlington Carmel.

In 1970, Sister Lucia's prioress encouraged her to write an article on Edith Stein for the *Catholic Herald*. It aroused considerable interest and one of the first letters she received was from Donald Nicholl. They kept in touch from then on.

In the mid-1970s Sister Lucia undertook the translation of a booklet by Sister Amata Neyer, *A Saint for our Times*, the first of several valuable publications by Neyer. She too, is a Carmelite sister, a member of the Cologne community, and is currently the Edith Stein archivist.

Printing has always been the major work of Darlington Carmel and so they were in a prime position to print this, together with two of Edith's short spiritual writings, *The Prayer of the Church* and *The Mystery of Christmas*. The former was translated by Sister Lucia and the latter by Sister Josephine Rucker, SSJ. At roughly the same time, Darlington printed a small booklet of *Reflections*, using a series of quotations and photographs from Edith's life. These were the first publications I was able to buy, and together with those I borrowed, and later owned, they formed the building blocks of my Edith library.

In 1992 Sister Lucia answered a call to join a new foundation in South Africa where she celebrated her Golden Jubilee in January 2002. Sister Lucia's modest contribution towards my jigsaw was, I remember, greatly prized by myself when there was so little available in the English language. Her translations, and Darlington's printing, brought Edith to the notice of many in England who might otherwise have remained unaware of her existence.

Misericordias Domini
in aeternum cantabo

In thanksgiving for the
grace of 50 years of
profession
in Carmel

1952 — 16 January — 2002
Darlington — Benoni

Sr Lucia of the Incarnation
(Mechthild Wiedenhöver)

Sister Lucia's Golden Jubilee, 2002: celebrating fifty years as a Carmelite.

* * * * *

An important stalk in this wreath of events and of people is an immediate connection between the Carmelite sisters of Cologne in Germany and those of Presteigne on the Welsh Borders. They both undertook the physical work of the restoration or building of their monastery and church. In the mid-1940s, immediately following the war, it was a time of great hardship. There was a profusion of vocations, money was short and buildings were essential to the future of the Order. It says much for the Carmelite vocation and surely the Teresian spirit that the sisters decided, and were able, quite literally to 'build' their own future.

The Carmelite chapel lay at the very heart of my new life in Presteigne. It was here that I encountered a Carmelite community at prayer for the first time. It was here that I found peace and tranquillity on my monthly hermit days. It was here that I made my first attempts to engage in a deeper prayer life. Not surprising, therefore, that I sought consolation 'here' as I continued on my stony path.

It has often crossed my mind that the history of this chapel would be better told by the bricks and mortar of which it is built. As I endeavour to do so on their behalf, I realize I am a mere onlooker glancing back in time. How was it that an unskilled workforce of women, wearing a Carmelite habit, was able to complete the building of a chapel, a little gem in its own right? We know the sisters were erecting a cloister and cells from basic materials such as railway sleepers. What gave them the notion they could move onto the greater skill of a brickwork building worthy of becoming the Lord's house? The notion was inspired by a postcard from Sister Renata of Cologne telling Mother Michael that her community intended to return to their first home in Cologne, 'Maria vom Frieden', Schnurgasse, where they would do the necessary rebuilding themselves. This was all the encouragement Mother Michael required in order to do the same.

Links between different Carmels around the world have always existed, never more so than immediately after the war, when many of them were endeavouring to put the pieces of their contemplative life back together again. How or why Mother Michael was in touch with Cologne I am uncertain.

Was it a continuation of the Sister Magdalen Spitz connection, I wonder? I like to think so.

In October 1944 the Cologne monastery of Lindenthal – where Edith entered Carmel and spent the first five years of her life as a Carmelite – was burned to the ground in a fierce air raid. The community escaped from the burning wreck, having spent the night in the cellar. One sister lost her life and the remainder of them found a temporary home in Augsburg. When the war was over the Cardinal encouraged Sister Renata and her community to return to their *first* home, the cradle of German Carmelites in the district of Schnurgasse where it was possible to repair the damaged church.

The Cologne sisters' first task was to clear the rubble, a result of the bomb damage. In a letter written to me in 1991 by Sister Christina, a member of the community, she says, 'Immediately after the war the sisters started to build up again the totally destroyed cloister and church, and of course, the material at that time was very bad. They did not even have an architect, just somebody who gave good tips. Many things and rooms now need repairs, some have to be changed because they are too small.' I gained the impression the latter referred to the entrance and extern quarters. I have no means of knowing how great the sisters' contribution to the rebuilding of the church may have been or whether in fact they built their own monastery unaided. I have learnt rather more about the building of the Presteigne church of Our Lady of the Assumption and St Thérèse.

In March 1951 the young architect Francis Pollen was working on the interior of a house close to Presteigne, for Lord Rennele of Rodd. His wife Lady Rennell, who was a devout Roman Catholic convert, took Francis to meet her new friend in Presteigne, none other than Mother Michael. The story goes that they found her in a bare room sanding down a statue of St Thérèse of Lisieux, 'taking off the lipstick' as she told them. When Mother Michael mentioned that the community planned to build their own chapel Francis immediately used the back of an envelope to provide some outline drawings. In the event he prepared full-scale designs for the building which he called 'nun-proof' and which he generously donated to the community. What a golden gift this was.

Francis Pollen was at the beginning of his illustrious career and went on to design bigger and greater buildings such as Worth Abbey and the octagonal library at Downside. In my estimation 'small is always beautiful' and the Carmelite chapel is a fine example of this. The Pollen 'nun-proof' plans were a simple design in the Italianate style which incorporated two-light windows with a circular light above, a scissor-truss roof with a skylight above the altar, two small windows either side of the tabernacle and a substantial rubble stone altar. On the west wall behind the altar is the great CHI RHO designed by the Welsh artist David Jones, a personal friend of Pollen's. A second design by the same artist, an inscription in both Welsh and Latin, was prepared for the east wall above the door in 1956, but was rejected as being too 'esoteric'.

The Presteigne community dug foundations, mixed concrete, cast lintels and window frames, laid brickwork and constructed and tiled the roof. A professional builder was called upon to construct the bellcote, a small concession to greater expertise. Stone was collected from the local quarry with the pony and trap and many economies were made along the way. It was an outstanding achievement and was the cause of considerable comment and approval. A film crew from BBC Cardiff were sufficiently interested to visit Presteigne and produced a revealing documentary, *Out of This World.*

When the Cologne sisters returned to Schnurgasse in 1949, the significance of Edith Stein and her life was little more than a whisper in the wind. Widely fêted in Germany for a few short years before the war, both as a lecturer and Doctor of Philosophy, Edith disappeared into the obscurity of Carmelite enclosure before becoming one of millions of Jews to die in Auschwitz. It is said that many within her own community were unaware of her stature as a Doctor of Philosophy. It was, of course, Sister Renata who first revealed her to many of us by writing her biography. In her 'Introduction' she writes: 'These pages are dedicated to the memory of a woman who radiated the light of truth in an age which loved darkness more than light. Therefore her life had to be extinguished by violence; but even in death she remained a confessor of the Truth, as the spirit of her immortal works will always show'. I believe Providence took a hand in the community's decision to return to the Schnurgasse. History was made here on two occasions centuries apart. It was here that the first Carmelites settled early in the seventeenth century and it was here that Edith said her last prayer for peace before leaving Germany in the twentieth century. It became a hallowed place of pilgrimage for me and, I am sure, for many others.

As 1985 merged into 1986 I continued to seek peace in my heart and to find contentment in my service of the Presteigne community. I often suffered emotionally by a visible lack of understanding, either by the community or myself, of my position at Carmel. It was so ill-defined. There were ups and downs aplenty. But a new friend can often be the salvation in difficult circumstances and this is how it was for me. Edith and her life provided me with an insight into suffering and how to deal with it. In my pain she became an understanding friend.

In April 1985 Sister Angela died and was the thirteenth sister buried in the Presteigne cemetery. In the same month Sister Edna celebrated her Diamond Jubilee, only to join Sister Angela in November 1986. She was the fourteenth and last member of the community to be laid to rest in the small cemetery. I knew Angela and Edna as old and infirm. In spite of their small stature they had been employed in the building of the monastery and the chapel. Diminutive they may have been, but nonetheless gallant in the pursuit of their vocation. They were a fine example of the 'worth' of this unconventional community.

It was a welcome encouragement to me when another candidate for the Third Order arrived in Presteigne. Susan Revill lived in Cardiff, where she was a hard-working doctor. She came to Carmel once a month for instruction with Sister Paddy and we soon became friends. Now there were two of us and I had someone of like mind with whom to share. At the same time I found my way to the Carmelite Priory at Oxford where I met further members from the Order and gradually began to feel less isolated.

As the Carmelite community diminished in numbers I was asked if I would undertake the post of sacristan. I was overjoyed at the prospect and while waiting for the sister in charge to hand over, I undertook the flower arrangements. I had and have no artistic skills but spent many hours trying to develop them! In the event the sacristan's job was passed to someone else. I was unable to hide my bitter disappointment as I continued with the weekly arrangement of the flowers.

Quite unexpectedly I became the only person living in the extern quarters in the middle of 1986. It set me thinking. Could I make the extern accommodation more attractive, less austere, and survive without regular escape to Combe Cottage? I discussed the situation with Sister Anne. We opened up the small, unused downstairs room. A solid fuel stove was installed, the walls were painted, I bought a few secondhand pieces of furniture, hung up some pictures and even rented a TV (which I had forgone since moving to Carmel). I let Combe Cottage for six months, to eliminate temptation. At the time it seemed like a massive step forward, but it worked. I became more settled and more able to cope with the ups and downs.

By now I was impatient for the long-promised English translation of Edith's autobiography, *Life in a Jewish Family*. I realized this would be my first opportunity to meet her face to face. In the meantime I applied myself to a third biography, *The Scholar and the Cross*, by Hilda Graef. This was published in 1955 by Longmans, Green & Co and cost 18s. It is a scholarly work and a touch less personal than the two I had already read. Hilda Graef, like Edith, was a German Jew. She came to England in 1936 and joined the Catholic Church in 1941. She enjoyed the advantage of having read both English and German literature and language at Berlin University before her arrival in England.

The Graef biography is obviously the result of meticulous research. She writes with an appreciation of Edith's philosophical mind and has at her hand Edith's two important works *Endliches und Ewiges Sein* (*Finite and Eternal Being*), not available in English until the end of 2002. And *Kreuzeswissenschaft* (*The Science of the Cross*) which Graef herself translated. *The Scholar and the Cross* greatly assisted my appreciation of the two concise spiritual writings printed by Darlington: *The Prayer of the Church* and *The Mystery of Christmas*.

The Prayer of the Church was written in 1936, the year following Edith's first profession as a Carmelite. Graef tells us it formed part of a symposium on 'The Stream of Life in the Church'. On this occasion Graef includes a long extract from the text to highlight Edith's blending of the Old Covenant with the New. At the same time Edith establishes the mutual relation between 'public' and 'private' prayer. The prayer of the lady who visited Frankfurt Cathedral with her shopping basket on her arm is as much part of the prayer of the Church as are prayers said in a community or by a large congregation. Graef believes Edith reveals a little of her hidden interior life when she uses the teaching of the Bible, the doctrines of the Church, and the guidance of the Spirit, in her own prayer life. She lays emphasis on Edith's breadth of vision that is never constrained by 'convent spirituality' – Graef's critique enabled me to appreciate Edith's writing at a deeper level than hitherto. I spent time with a more inclusive translation of *The Prayer of the Church* which appeared in The Collected Works of Edith Stein, Volume 4 (*The Hidden Life*) and I am pleased to return to this for further meditation time and again.

The Mystery of Christmas is of similar length and was delivered as a lecture to Catholic academics in January 1931. It provides a profound bittersweet meditation on Christmas. The star, the Advent hymns, the O antiphons surround us in the bliss of Christmas, only for that bliss to be closely followed by the martyrdom of Stephen and the slaughter of the Innocents. 'Thus the road from Bethlehem leads irresistibly to Golgotha, from the manger to the cross,' Edith tells us. 'To suffer and to die is the lot of every human being,' but 'He knows our nature; he takes it into consideration and therefore he has given us everything which can help us to reach our goal.' What comforting words those are. Towards the end of the paper she tells us, 'In the dark of Good Friday the light is extinguished, but it rises more brightly as the sun of Grace on the morning of the Resurrection.' There is no better companion during Christmastide than this short treatise of Edith's.

Graef devotes an entire chapter of nearly twenty pages to *Finite and Eternal Being*. I question whether I will ever be able fully to comprehend Edith's deep philosophical writings. The jury is still out. I intend buying a translated edition and will then return to Graef's Chapter 18, knowing that it will provide a helpful, guiding hand. Graef is quite critical of Edith's last work *The Science of the Cross* and suggests she may not have had the best literature available to assist her undertaking. Be that as it may, we certainly should not dismiss Edith's final *opus* on this single opinion. Readers more qualified than I will form their own judgement as and when they read the latest translation by Josephine Koeppel.

CHAPTER FOUR

1987 - An Extraordinary Year

A translation of *Life in a Jewish Family* was finally published by ICS Publications, Washington in 1986, and is Volume 1 of The Collected Works of Edith Stein, subtitled *Her Unfinished Autobiographical Account*. It is edited by Dr Lucy Gelber and Romaeus Leuven, OCD and translated by Josephine Koeppel, OCD. I bought a copy towards the end of 1986. It cost me £8.95. A short 'Introduction' by the chairman of ICS, John Sullivan, OCD, is followed by a 'Preface' to the unabridged German edition in 1963, by Romaeus Leuven. A shorter preface by Dr Gelber, dated January 1985, confirms this is a complete edition. An 'Editors' Foreword' describes the archival papers from which the text is translated and contains reminiscences, written by Edith's sister Erna, in 1949. The book comprises ten chapters with a short 'Foreword' written by Edith when she began the work in 1933. It is a fat volume with a limp cover. My copy soon appeared well worn.

I had coveted this book for so long. I was not disappointed. It is a transparent and faithful account of the fabric of the extended Stein family. For this reason some members of Edith's family were unhappy at being portrayed in a less than favourable light. Edith could only ever be truthful and this is how her story reads without malice, but as things were in the Stein household. Chapter one has the title 'My Mother Remembers' and Edith writes, 'If I must record in these pages some matters which may appear to my dear brothers and sisters as criticism of their weaknesses, they will forgive me.

One cannot write about a mother's life without going into all she experienced with her children and suffered because of them. When, eventually, my turn comes, I will not come away less scorched than the others.'

In order fully to appreciate this autobiography, it is as well to read the 'Editors' Foreword'. It is a description of the original one thousand pages, written in Latin script in Edith's neat hand, often on one side only, using corrected sheets from her students' notebooks. The story of the manuscript's journey from Cologne to Echt, the time it spent in the Echt monastery graveyard and cellar, before eventually arriving in the safekeeping of the Carmelite Order, has been told before. It is Father Romaeus, OCD and Dr Lucy Gelber whom we have to thank for a meticulous and scholarly work in preparing the biography for publication. And beyond them Josephine Koeppel, OCD who is responsible for the English translation. You cannot undertake work of this nature without becoming close to your subject. I am sure they all did, and in doing so, they have enabled me to do so, these many years later. In life, Edith had many enduring friendships. She does so again in death.

Before continuing with my enjoyment of the book I must mention the 'Chronology', 'Translator's Afterword', 'Notes' and comprehensive 'Index' provided by Josephine Koeppel, OCD. They occupy one hundred and thirty-two pages at the end of the autobiography. As I began a serious study of Edith's life, I often appreciated the value of this exhaustive supplement.

When *Life in a Jewish Family* finally came into my possession I was unable to put it down. I was totally absorbed and many of my own problems melted away as I found myself walking beside Edith. It is a potent blend of family and friends, study and service, suffering and joy, and is rarely short on detail. The ten chapters do not take us beyond 1916, Edith's twenty-fifth year. For the remainder of her life we have to depend on the evidence of those who knew her and her published letters. The latter were not available in English until 1993.

Edith provides a very clear picture of herself as a wilful, disturbed small child, as an independent, precocious teenager and as a dedicated student at university. We are aware of the close bond she had with her mother and with her sister Erna. We learn how her many friendships are intertwined with her love of philosophy, the arts and the countryside. Her experience of nursing in the war, the strains of an excessive self-imposed workload, a self-confessed vivid imagination and her enjoyment of special occasions, are all part and parcel of Edith's illuminating autobiography.

I have chosen a short quotation, from chapter five, which encapsulates so well the twenty-year-old Edith, as a student at Breslau. 'During free periods, I liked to study in an empty lecture room; there I would seat myself on one of the wide window sills which filled the deep recesses in the wall. Looking down from such a lofty perch at the river and the busy University Bridge, I could imagine myself to be maiden in her castle ... There, in a world of silence and peace, I felt transplanted into long-gone centuries.'

My favourite chapter, 'Student Years in Göttingen', is number seven. It is here that Edith is fulfilled in study, in friendship, in appreciation of the city she loved so well and in the philosophical backdrop to daily life. At one point she writes, 'Besides, I had come to Göttingen for no more than that summer, and I counted on taking the state boards in Breslau. Granted, the closer we came to the end of the semester, the more intolerable I found the thought of having to go away and not returning. The months gone by were not just an episode, after all, but rather the beginning of a new phase of my life.' In the event, Edith returned to Göttingen to continue her studies and visited friends there on many occasions in subsequent years. Göttingen always held a very special place in her heart.

* * * * *

To take the leap from Edith's *Life in a Jewish Family* to beatification on 1 May 1987 – a full seventy years after the events described – is almost too big a leap to take. But this is how it was for me. As I sat in the garden at Combe Cottage (my tenants had left in mid-April) on 1 May, a glorious sunny Friday, my thoughts and spirit were far away in Cologne knowing that the Pope was there to beatify Edith Stein. I spent the day reading her autobiography and becoming closer to her page by page. It was the next best thing to being in Cologne.

It was on this day I first wrote a note in my diary, 'I have a dream of sharing what Edith means to me with others.'

When I opened the newspapers the following morning, I realized the life of Edith Stein was no longer confined to her homeland. The beatification produced a storm from the leader writers, who questioned the wisdom of the Church. Was it wise, they asked, to raise so controversial a figure to a status just short of sainthood? An article in the *Catholic Herald* prior to the beatification read, 'A Martyr for which Faith?' and the day following 1 May two headlines read, 'Behind a Strange Martyrdom' and 'The Pope and Doctor Stein'. Her life-story was analyzed and different views were expressed. Most of it saddened me and took some of the gilt off this memorable day.

Sometime after the event Father John Sullivan, OCD wrote 'Most noteworthy in hindsight is the double qualification with which Stein's cause for beatification concluded, i.e., approval of her heroic virtues as well as approval of her martyrdom ... one would have welcomed a decision by the Vatican authorities to include the other Catholics who met their deaths with her.' This would, of course, have embraced her sister Rosa, Alice Reis and many others, all of whom were her 'companions' on the journey to Auschwitz.

It was the Carmelite community of Cologne who had taken the first steps towards Edith's beatification. Immediately after the war they began collecting documentation relating to Edith's life. The Posselt biography was a direct result. In 1958 the Archbishop of Cologne, Cardinal Frings, received permission from the Vatican for initial steps to be taken to investigate her life, virtues and writings. A shorter draft of the Posselt was prepared and was supported by five volumes of Edith's works which were published in Belgium between 1950 and 1958. In 1962, Cardinal Frings opened the Ordinary Process, to be followed by the Apostolic Process. Help was enlisted from other dioceses and sworn statements were taken from Dr Erna Biberstein, Edith's sister, and individuals in twenty-two cities around the world. As is always the case, it was a lengthy process and eventually in 1972 Cardinal Höffner (Frings' successor) sent the material to Rome. In 1986 a new brief to go beyond the question of heroic virtues, to investigate martyrdom, was included. The Decree confirming this was promulgated in January 1987 and her beatification followed on 1 May the same year.

Neyer's booklet, *A Saint for our Times,* assists us when weighing the pros and cons of Edith's beatification. She writes, 'It has been God's good pleasure that [Edith Stein] should not remain unknown.' She tells us that holiness is the decisive factor in any beatification but suggests that, as a woman of modern thought and feeling, Edith has special relevance for our time. The fact that she was a professional, long before she was a Carmelite, dispels the notion of 'just another nun'. 'It is the significance of Edith Stein's destiny as a Jewess, not as a Carmelite, that we are considering . . . Why single out this one [Jew] from amongst the many others who met their death in Auschwitz? . . . Because this single one stands in the place of them all.'

Daniel Johnson wrote in *The Daily Telegraph* on 1 May, 'The Blessed Teresa Benedicta of the Cross, as she will henceforth be invoked in prayer, was a martyr both to her faith, which was Catholic, and to her people, who were Jewish. Only those who have not troubled to understand the works and the personality of this supremely gifted and profoundly troubled woman, will deny the dual symbolism of her life.' This is a fitting response to those who question Edith's place in the Church.

Shortly after the beatification, the BBC 1 *Everyman* series produced a half-hour documentary. A panel of four were invited to discuss the topic. They were Rabbi Hugo Gryn, a survivor of Auschwitz; Cordelia Edvardson who had been in Auschwitz as a child and who had converted from Christianity to Judaism; a Sister of Sion; and Robert Sarno. Edith's life and work were given scant attention. The focus was almost entirely directed towards the Catholic Church from the Jewish perspective. Their sentiments were already bruised with the building of a Carmelite Convent at Auschwitz, together with a large cross overlooking the railway. They accused the Church of beatifying a 'turncoat' and of attempting to hijack the Holocaust. Nonetheless I was impressed by Cordelia's testimony and the sheer cheerful goodness of Hugo Gryn. In his obituary – which I read some years later – I learnt that his stock phrase was, 'Tell me nice things.' The suffering in Auschwitz had taught this good man the strength and value of prayer. As a pastor, teacher and friend he was much loved. The *Everyman* discussion concluded with agreement. Prayer, made in the spirit of 'being there with those who have gone before', must be welcomed, no matter what religion those who pray, in this spirit, belong to.

More important than the general discussion and comment was the Holy Father's visit to Germany and his message to the people while there. On the day he arrived in Cologne he addressed the German bishops and said, 'Edith Stein is a shining example to us in this pursuit of spiritualization.' He made the following important point: 'she was a daughter of the Jewish people. In solidarity with them, and in Christian hope she shared their sufferings on the way to Shoah.'

In his homily at the beatification the Pope quoted Cardinal Höffner when he said, 'Edith Stein is a gift, an invocation and a promise for our time. May she be an intercessor with God for us and for our people and for all people.' On the same day he met the Jewish Central Council and to them he said, 'today the church is honouring a daughter of Israel who remained faithful, as a Jew, to the Jewish people, and, as a Catholic, to our crucified Lord Jesus Christ.' In the afternoon he visited Münster in recognition of the time Edith had spent as a lecturer at the Münster Institute for Scientific Pedagogy. Each of the Pope's visits was rich in symbolism and thanksgiving.

On Sunday 3 May, the Holy Father visited Munich to beatify the Jesuit priest Father Rupert Mayer. In the evening of the same day he celebrated Mass in Augsburg for the people of the Diocese.

Finally, on the afternoon of 4 May, the Holy Father arrived in Speyer, Edith's home for eight years when teaching at St Magdalena's Dominican College. The Holy Father celebrated Mass in the large square in front of Speyer Cathedral and urged the people to be 'faithful guardians of [Edith's] message and of her life testimony.' The people of Speyer took the Holy Father's words to heart and the Edith Stein Society of Germany was formed there. Their regular meetings and newsletters ensure that Edith's life and works are kept alive and active. Had the Holy Father been able to travel to Breslau, Göttingen, Freiburg and Echt he would have completed Edith's life circle. As it was he honoured a new figure in the

Church, one whose message was relevant for the twentieth century and the millennium beyond. We may be sure His Holiness felt an affinity with and a special regard for Edith, having studied phenomenology under her fellow student, Roman Ingarden, in his youth.

A stamp was issued in Germany to commemorate the beatification in 1987 of Edith Stein in Cologne and Rupert Mayer, SJ in Munich. It was a portrait of their heads side by side.

* * * * *

Earlier in the year, on 25 March 1987, Presteigne Carmel celebrated Sister Paddy's Silver Jubilee. It was a very special day with members of Paddy's large family travelling from the North of Ireland to share it with her. One of the community 'oldies', Sister Monica, celebrated sixty years of Carmelite life in her own inimitable way in April, and Sister Bernadette her Silver Jubilee in July. I, the guestmistress, felt woefully inadequate on these big occasions. My morale sank even lower when some relatives preferred to stay with the erstwhile guestmistress in Presteigne or at the Radnor Arms. Nonetheless it was good to share these happy occasions amidst an ongoing search for the future of the community. I was, of course, not party to their discussions but was not unaware of them. A visit by the prioress of the Cape Town community in South Africa signified that something fundamental was being considered.

In May I was asked to drive a darling old sister, Mary Assumpta, to a retirement home run by religious in Colwyn Bay. Most of her Carmelite life had been spent as a lay sister in another Carmel. Presteigne welcomed her as a choir sister and her joy in the use of the breviary, and indeed her own tuneful voice, was there for all to see and hear. As she aged and suffered indifferent health it was decided she required greater care than she could receive in Carmel. Colwyn Bay was not a success and we fetched her home. In July I drove her all the way to Hawick, on the Scottish borders, where she settled happily and stayed until she died nearly two years later.

Early in the year Susan and I were joined in the Third Order by Chris Hemson. Chris is a married mother of two who lives near Hereford. She was like a breath of fresh air. We became the three musketeers, each with a strong commitment to Carmel. The friendship between us kept this alive during a long period of relative isolation from the First and Second Orders.

Plans were under way for my visit to Germany towards the end of September. I had been invited to judge at the Connemara pony show at Kargen in Bavaria. I was to stay with my friends, Edith and Beatrice Milleder, in Munich but my journey began with a flight to Frankfurt where the Hillnhutter family met me. Beatrice arrived by road the following day. Our drive from Frankfurt to Munich was arranged in order for me to visit Cologne Carmel en route. Yet once again my Connemara and Carmelite interests were coming together, thanks to the kindness of the Milleders.

The ivy which binds my wreath together is provided by several Carmelite friars. I first met Father John Hughes when making plans for my visit to Germany in 1987. He sent me the address and telephone number of Cologne Carmel and an unusual drawing of Edith together with a postcard. The drawing is a bare pen and ink study of the back view of a person (Edith) seated at a desk with pen in hand and a tidy stack of papers nearby. There are empty tables beyond with the focus funnelling in on a central shaft of light with opening shutters either side and a cross above. I am sure it could be described, interpreted and meditated upon in a variety of ways. Father John had recently returned from Cologne, having attended Edith's beatification. He encouraged my interest in her but wrote, 'I doubt Edith Stein will ever be popular. She is such a tragic figure, but I have felt attracted to that face so full of pathos.' Father John studied Edith's life when using her doctoral thesis on empathy as the subject for his *Tesina* for the degree of S.T.L. at the Teresianum, Rome. It is an excellent exposé of her work.

I subsequently attended two retreats at Boars Hill directed by Father John on Edith's life and work, in 1988 and again in 1994. Each one brought me a little closer to appreciating her many and often hidden qualities. His introduction on the first occasion was a sketch of Breslau and the life of the Stein household in the late nineteenth and early twentieth centuries, which he described as 'the balmy days of European life, a strange and far-off world before the outbreak of World War

Two.' We learnt how Edith's conversion to Christianity was incomprehensible to her family, and how such a person was regarded as 'dead' in Jewish circles. Edith was able to overcome their lack of understanding by remaining constant in her love for them all. Father John traced her academic career and her conversion. Reading St Teresa's life was not, he told us, the main source of her conversion but provided the final ounce. Her life in Carmel was one of obedience where her prayer became a 'silent sermon'.

He offered some new insights into the person and nature of Edith in his second retreat in 1994 and I came away with two or three salient points. 'Catholicism divided their minds but not their hearts [referring to Edith and her family]. Baptism did not separate her [Edith] from the God of Israel and so she was able to pray beside her mother in the synagogue – grace builds on nature – the goal and way of human existence is the theme of Edith's writing – no one can make himself into what he is not – Edith's birth date set the theme for her life [the Day of Atonement].' There was of course much, much more. It is likely each one of us returned home stimulated by the three days with a better understanding of our new, multi-faceted saint for our times.

During the days of sharing Edith with Father John during the 1988 retreat he became my friend 'in waiting'. I had good reason to be grateful to him when suddenly and unexpectedly in 1993 I hit a personal crisis. I happened to be at Boars Hill and who better to turn to in my distress than a friend of Edith's? Thanks to Father John's wise counsel I returned to Combe Cottage having regained my peace of mind.

The 1994 retreat was important for another very good reason. I met Joanne Mosley for the first time. I had little idea what an important 'daisy' she would become in the years ahead. On this occasion we exchanged addresses before leaving Boars Hill and vowed to keep in touch. Joanne told me she spoke German and kindly offered to translate some of my German correspondence.

In 1992 a similar retreat was led by a layperson, Philippa Burrows. The retreat centre was full. The opportunity to study St Teresa of Avila, St John of the Cross or Edith Stein had encouraged bookings. In the event few wanted to join the Edith group and three were diverted from St John, by agreement, to bring our number to six. It was apparent Edith had not yet gathered a 'following' among many with Carmelite interests. Philippa was a good leader and brought a disparate small group happily together in company with Edith.

In September 1987 Father Nicholas Madden, OCD was invited to Presteigne to conduct the annual community retreat. As guestmistress I shared meals with him and was concerned with his general well-being. From time to time I felt privileged when invited to attend conferences given to the community by visiting clergy. Never more so than on this occasion. The talks invited me to share a far deeper understanding of scripture and Carmelite spirituality than hitherto. He soon became a friend and we were 'granted' a free day by the prioress which we spent exploring the Welsh hills, Capel-y-Ffin and Llanthony and the bookshops of Hay-on-Wye. Father Nicholas has a scholarly mind; for many years he taught at the seminary in Carlow, and his lectures and company stimulated my unexposed 'dry matter'. His appreciation of Edith's writings took me beyond my personal study of her life and character.

In 1992 I was at Boars Hill for a weekend of sharing 'The Passover' in company with Rabbi Lionel Blue and Father Nicholas. It was a riveting experience as one bounced off the other and the Old and the New Covenant were explored and, I might add, 'lived' side by side. The two perspectives and beliefs were examined in good humour, while the Passover meal, which we all shared, was an unforgettable encounter. Father Nicholas sat beside the Rabbi wearing a similar small black skullcap with a twinkle in his eye. The Rabbi led us through the 'Seder' step by step, the egg, the bitter herbs, the shank bone, the parsley, the salt and horseradish sauce, all symbolic signs of the coming out of Egypt to begin a new life. He explained how the Jews did not want another heroic leader like Moses, they wished for freedom and believed laws were for a living community and not for dead heroes. He told us we are all children of Abraham but for Jews it is difficult to understand Christianity. Nonetheless Rabbi Blue has for many years been a regular visitor to Boars Hill and a friend of the community.

Father Nicholas portrayed Christ as the priest and victim of the New Covenant who brings his sacrificial death with him in the Eucharist. He is the lamb who was slain on the eve of the Passover meal. Our religion is something we live by, while God remains a mystery. The weekend led me to a better understanding of the chasm that exists between Judaism and Christianity, and the reality of the cost to Edith, and others like her, to cross it.

Father Nicholas remains a close friend, but we meet all too rarely. His health is poor and he resides in Dublin but his support, understanding and friendship are, I feel, never far away.

During the course of my ten days in Germany I travelled many hundreds of miles, judged ponies for two days in pouring rain, and walked into and out of Edith Stein's world on three occasions, all the time suffering from a heavy cold. Memories of the notable milestones in my 'discovery of Edith Stein' realized in 1987 are described in Chapter five.

I returned to Presteigne Carmel on 30 September to the usual round of chores, a visit from my mother, who lived in Hampshire, a dash to Boarbank for the Requiem of a dearly loved Augustinian sister, a parish bazaar, Chris Hemson's reception for formation into the Secular Order and a Connemara judges' seminar, all the while preparing for a visit to South Africa. It seemed a surreal world in which I was moving.

The journey to South Africa was a result of the visit to Presteigne from the prioress of Wynberg Carmel in Cape Town earlier in the year. I never fully understood, neither did I ask, the ramifications of the South Africa 'idea'. The possibility of two diminished Carmels, one in South Africa and the other on the Welsh Borders, amalgamating in a new building in South Africa was, I believe, being considered, unlikely a proposition as this may sound. Sister Anne planned an exploratory mission. My goddaughter lived in Cape Town. A visit to her while Anne was at Carmel suggested I would be a suitable travelling companion. The journey became an expedition once Johannesburg and Lesotho were added to the itinerary of our improbable excursion.

Rather misguidedly, Anne was in touch with the Carmel in Athens before we left. Our tickets included overnight hotel accommodation in Athens where the airline broke our long flight. We were met at the airport by a friend of the Carmel who insisted we stay with them. It required a taxi to take us right out of the city and I became more and more anxious about our return early next morning. The extern quarters had been prepared for us and reeked of mothballs. I doubt it had been used in the last decade. The community was small in number. They welcomed our visit with such obvious pleasure that the mothballs were soon forgotten. We only connected with our flight next morning by a whisker and I felt shattered by the whole experience. On our arrival in Cape Town we had to catch a train to Johannesburg.

The train journey across South Africa, part of which was through the night, was memorable. The stay in Johannesburg was brief. All I saw of the great city was shopping malls but Anne had a happy visit to Rivonia Carmel where she was made most welcome. On our return to Cape Town, my goddaughter met us at the airport and drove Anne to the Carmel. I spent three happy days with Seonaid and her family. I have memories of the final day on which we visited Table Mountain. The heat was blistering and I felt in danger of sunstroke with nothing to cover my head. That night I went to bed with a slight temperature. It was not a good moment to be feeling under the weather. Early the next morning I was due to catch a flight to Blomfontein.

My friend Donal Kenny had arrived in Africa from Ireland a day or so earlier. He met me at Blomfontein airport and my excitement was intense as we sped across the plains of Africa on our way to the land-locked tiny kingdom of Lesotho. There was strict control at the border. An armed guard in army uniform studiously inspected our passports before applying the Maseru stamp of approval. I was about to realize a long-held interest in the Basotho pony project with a visit to Thaba Teska.

Early in the 1980s the Irish government undertook, as a Third World project, the regeneration of the Basotho pony breed. It had been sorely depleted as a consequence of the Boer War. Donal was responsible for putting the plan into action and two Connemara stallions were sent from Ireland to assist the breeding programme. When you drive high into the mountains of Lesotho you realize how important the pony is to the everyday life of the Lesotho people. It is their main and often only means of transport.

A modern stable block had been built, the surrounding land was divided into small enclosures, the local natives were trained in stud management and the best mares were hand-picked to run with the Connemara stallions.

Lesotho is the Africa you read and dream about with an indigenous native population who live by their age-old customs. The men and women alike wear multi-coloured blankets that provide protection from both the heat and the cold. On their head they wear a conical shaped straw hat and their seat aboard the Basotho pony is that of one who grew up on horseback. The majestic mountains, the ravines with waterfalls tumbling in torrents to bubbling streams below are wild beauty beyond compare. Johannesburg's shopping malls and the Table Mountain's cable car belong to a different world.

I spent one night in my friend John's small box-like house. He was away from home and I was able to stem my rising temperature with glasses of iced water throughout the night. The following day Donal took me to the Roma mission hospital where tests revealed a kidney infection. By this time I felt very rough and spent a day in bed in a Blomfontein hotel before we began the long flight home. Nothing very positive had emerged from Anne's Carmelite visits but she returned with food for thought.

CHAPTER FIVE

Cologne - Dachau - Beuron

Frankfurt Airport was bewilderingly large and busy and I was grateful to see Mrs Hillnhutter's familiar face among the waiting crowd. I was driven to a small comfortable hotel where I spent two nights. The following morning I realized I was in the throes of a heavy cold that I did not manage to shake off for several days. Beatrice and I began the long drive to Munich via Cologne early on 23 September. I could hardly believe that a visit to Cologne Carmel was only a drive away. My friends in Frankfurt had kindly telephoned the Carmel and arranged for me to meet Sister Amata Neyer.

Beatrice insisted we should visit Cologne Cathedral before trying to find the Carmel. Of course, she was right to overrule my impatience to meet Sister Amata. Cologne Cathedral is not a place to be bypassed. The *Dom* is a mighty Gothic building that dominates the city and it has a long and noble history. The foundation stone was laid in 1258 and the construction was achieved during two periods, the first ending in 1560 and the second in 1880. The shrine of The Three Holy Magi, the colourful Bible windows, the huge statue of St Christopher carrying the Christ Child and the Baroque altar of the Cross are only four of the many beauties of this magnificent cathedral. Most of the war damage had been repaired before our visit and one can only believe a miracle saved it from total destruction.

To find the Carmel was not easy. Being used, as I am, to English Carmels, I was looking for a large house behind a high wall, but Beatrice assured me we would find the entrance on a busy street. And so we did, a simple brass plate on the wall: *Kloster Maria vom Frieden, Karmelitinnen* and a doorbell beside it. We were greeted by a Carmelite sister who directed us to the crypt and who told us Sister Amata would meet us in the parlour when we were ready.

The crypt is designed as a shrine or memorial to Edith and indeed to all former members of the Cologne community. Each one is identified by a small cross on the wall with the sister's name and relevant dates. A mould of Edith's head is placed on an altar beneath a crucifix and an inscribed tablet on the wall provides brief details of her life and death. To one side is a wrought-iron screen and a gold-leaf candle on which Edith's full-length figure, in her habit, is imposed. Her Jewish heritage is acknowledged by a simple embroidered 'hanging' depicting a candelabrum holding seven candles. Discreet dried-flower decorations on the altar, wall and screen lighten the sombre surroundings. A bench and prie-dieu are available for those wishing to spend time in prayer.

As I prayed, my thoughts drifted to the late December night in 1938, when Edith made her final prayer for peace on German soil. It was at her own request that her driver took her to the Schnurgasse in order that she might pray before the statue of Our Lady of Peace. She was on her way to the Carmel of Echt in The Netherlands. Neither the statue nor Edith herself survived the ravages of war.

Beatrice was incredibly patient as I endeavoured to soak up the atmosphere of this place of remembrance. Would I ever be lucky enough to visit Cologne again, I wondered.

On our return to the extern quarters we were shown to a roomy parlour where we met a seminal figure in my wreath of discovery, Sister Amata Neyer. My memories of her are very clear. A small neat figure with a cherubic countenance and a winning smile. She wore glasses and the old-style toque beneath her veil. She made us most welcome and spoke fast at great length - in German, of course - to Beatrice. She told us a little about herself but more about Edith and the day of her beatification. As she did so, tears of emotion welled in her bright little eyes and her small expressive hands indicated the depth of her feeling as she recalled this special occasion. From time to time Beatrice acted as interpreter and relayed questions and answers back and forth between us. How I wished I spoke German.

In 2002 Sister Amata celebrated her eightieth birthday, and as she is Edith's archivist this was reported in the Cologne church newspaper, together with some facts about her life. Marianne Neyer was born in Cologne on Easter Sunday, 1922. She has a twin sister, and her two brothers became priests. Marianne began medical studies on leaving school in 1940 but was already considering the possibility of a vocation to religious life. She entered Carmel when the Cologne sisters were in Augsburg and took her final vows in 1949, once the community had returned to Cologne. She was elected prioress in 1961 and on six further occasions up to 1988. Sister Amata undertook the task as archivist of Edith's life and works in 1964 and has continued this work ever since. She maintains that she could now tell you more or less where Edith was and what she was writing on any given day of her life. How grateful we have to be to this 'daisy' for her love of Edith and her supreme dedication to the preservation of her life and work.

Our drive to Munich took several hours, during the first half of which Beatrice recounted her long conversation with Sister Amata. What a memory she has! When we finally arrived at Am Brombeerschlag, we were both weary and ready for bed. The following day, Beatrice, and her mother, Edith, had to prepare their ponies for the show. In their thoughtfulness, they arranged to leave me at Dachau Carmel whilst they were busy. I believe I may have suggested a visit to Auschwitz, when they asked where my interests lay. This was not accessible but Dachau was.

This, the first concentration camp built by the Third Reich in 1933, is situated on the outskirts of Dachau and was divided into thirty barracks intended to accommodate 5,000 prisoners. It was often the case that between twelve and twenty thousand were housed there. In the space of twelve years more than 200,000 prisoners died in Dachau. In 1945 the prisoners who remained were liberated. Fifteen years later more than 40,000 people assembled for the blessing of a monument of atonement. At the same time, a chapel was dedicated to The Agony of Christ. The impressive circular tower built of stone has a large metal crown of thorns hanging over the entrance. A crucifix dominates the interior. The monument was blessed during the 37th Eucharistic World Congress of Munich. In his sermon Bishop Hengsbach said:

> The decisive factor in our readiness to make atonement is that we believe in the strength of the grain of wheat, which if it falls into the earth and dies, brings forth much fruit. And because of this awareness, our expiatory prayer must include this thought: In our striving towards justice in the world and for peace and harmony among nations and peoples, let us realize that salvation and healing come only from the Cross and merits of Our Lord Jesus Christ and be convinced that force alone will never achieve true peace.

It was this thought that gave birth to the foundation of the Carmel of 'Heilig-Blut' (Precious Blood) at Dachau.

The approach to the Carmelite courtyard passes through an old watchtower on the north side of the camp. The Carmel was designed and built in the form of a cross and has the appearance of a cloak spread over the hermits whose cells have been built together. They all face southwards towards the former concentration camp. The choir, in a central position with a red roof, occupies three times as much space. The belfry has three bells: the largest is called the 'Blood of Christ' bell; the one in the centre is dedicated to the Mother of God and St Teresa; the small bell is the one which was used at Stadelheim to announce the executions. The Carmelites ring these bells at 3.00 p.m. every day for prayers for the dying, and again at 6.00 p.m. after the Angelus for all the faithful departed. On the northern side of the convent there is a large garden where wild flowers and trees have been planted around two fishponds. In traditional fashion the sisters grow and harvest their own vegetables and fruit. This then is where I came, on a September day in 1987.

On my arrival I found I was expected and was directed to a large room in which were scattered small tables and chairs. It was the sisters' parlour where they met their guests. No grille or barriers in sight. Sister Christa, who spoke excellent English, spent some time with me expressing interest in my work with an English Carmel and my attraction to Edith Stein and her life. She took me to their shop, in which there were many attractive items, most of which were the sisters' own handiwork. They were skilled in the making of vestments, icons, rosaries and the like. I was invited to join the community for Vespers where the laity shared the sisters' choir rather than, as is usually the case, being segregated the other side of a grille. I found this sharing and informality between the sisters and their guests in choir and in the parlour effectual and welcome in a place overloaded with heavy symbolism. I do not doubt that our presence praying 'beside them' was as meaningful to them as to us. We were there to share their offering of atonement, even if only briefly.

The guests' dining room was plainly furnished with a long oak table in the centre, around which I and three other guests sat for a shared meal. It was an interesting small group. A young German girl, an American gentleman, a sister from the John Bosco congregation and myself. To my relief, we were able to converse in English and shared an interesting discussion.

Perhaps it was just as well I did not have the opportunity to walk around what remains of the foundations of the camp, or to visit the museum, or to experience the sense of desolation and death behind the high walls wreathed in barbed wire. I left with the sense of prayer, of hospitality and of peace that the presence of a Carmelite community has brought to this former death camp. As I walked away from Dachau I did not carry painful memories of suffering and death but rather I marvelled at the wonder and strength of Carmelite prayer and its healing presence.

The sisters came together at Dachau in the early 1960s. There has been no opposition to their presence. Sadly, the same cannot be said for the Carmel founded in Auschwitz in 1984. This provoked such angry protest that the Pope himself had to intervene and ask the sisters to move.

When writing about the Carmelite vocation in *The Science of the Cross* Edith Stein says:

> What is demanded here is not merely a small degree of withdrawal from the world, a certain improvement in this or that circumstance, praying a little longer, or practicing a little renunciation while at the same time enjoying consolations and spiritual feelings.
>
> Those who wish to satisfy themselves with this much will

> 'run as from death itself' 'as soon as they encounter something of this solid perfection that consists of the annihilation of all sweetness in God, in dryness, distaste, and trial. This is the purely spiritual cross and nakedness of poverty in the spirit of Christ.' The other is 'nothing other than the seeking of oneself in God - something entirely contrary to love' ... our goal is union with God, our way that of the crucified Christ, our becoming one with him takes place when we are crucified. The only proportionate means to arrive at this union is faith.

This, I believe, is what I experienced at the Carmel of 'Heilig-Blut'.

The following day I returned to the main purpose of my visit to Germany, the judging of Connemara ponies. It was not easy to switch focus so dramatically from Dachau to the job in hand. Another long drive from Munich to Kargen provided the opportunity to do so and, by the next day, I was ready for the task ahead of me. A beautiful showground site and an interesting selection of ponies were overshadowed by incessant, penetrating rain. The organizers ensured the day continued as planned and exhibitors, ponies, judges and spectators saw it through with great resolution. Hopeless, as I am, in the use of a shower I could only find cold water and discovered that beer, and not a hot toddy was the liquid on offer, together with hotdogs, hardly my favourite sustenance. My cold continued to take its course. The Milleders and I returned to Munich the next day, somewhat dejected and rather the worse for wear.

Ironically, the sun was shining when we crawled out of our beds the following morning. I was spending one more day in Munich and I wondered if the Milleders had anything planned. By now, Beatrice had my cold and her mother had not been too well the evening before. This did not deter her from saying after breakfast: 'Now we will go to Beuron' and this is exactly what we did. I could not believe I had another 'Edith day' ahead of me and I can never fully express my gratitude to the Milleders for the generous giving of their time to fulfil my every wish.

As we sped westward, we paid a brief visit to the Roman town of Augsburg, Edith Milleder's home town. It was a relief not to be travelling on the German *Autobahns* and to enjoy the beautiful countryside bathed in rich autumn colours. I was tingling with excitement and anticipation.

Beuron Abbey occupies a commanding spot in the upper Danube Valley sitting as it does:

> on a terrace a little above the valley floor, around which the Danube flows in wide bends from west to east. Steep slopes surround the valley, and the forest is often interrupted by cliffs of the Swabian Jura, which give the landscape its heroic-romantic appearance.

Founded in 1077 by the Order of Augustinian Canons, the Abbey subsequently suffered the distress of the Thirty Years War and later still the effects of the French Wars. It was not until 1853 that it passed into the hands of the Benedictines. From the beginning, it was placed under the protection of the Blessed Virgin and St Martin of Tours.

I am not romantic by nature but on this occasion I became so. We parked the car alongside the Danube, which separated us from the driveway to the Abbey, and walked across the majestic, ancient, covered, wooden bridge, which spans the great river. Pedestrians alone may use this access, though in days past, horses and coaches regularly drove across its broad timbers. I instinctively began to walk fast - Edith was said always to walk 'fast'! As we passed the lodge in which she stayed when visiting for Holy Week and Easter, I realized this would have been her approach to the Abbey as she made her way to join the monks for early morning prayer. I could feel the slim intense figure hurrying along beside me as I looked ahead at the Abbey glistening in early evening sunlight soon after 4.00 p.m. We might, I thought, be in time for Vespers - if we hurried. On enquiring in the Abbey shop - the first building we came to - we were told Solemn Vespers had been said at 3.00 p.m. The monks celebrate the Anniversary of the Dedication of the Abbey - which took place in 1738 - on 28 September each year - today! Disappointing, but now at least we had the Abbey to ourselves.

The guidebook to the Abbey writes of the inside as 'festively decorated', with ceiling frescoes, paintings, pictures and ornaments, wood carvings, altar screens, Baroque art and angel figures. Biblical stories are vividly portrayed, as are many of the saints of the Church, with special attention given to St Martin of Tours. A high altar and two side altars are constructed with stucco marble pillars. I did not consider it ornate or yet opulent or overcrowded. It evokes the history of 'the Church' in beauty and craftsmanship. You feel welcome in a pervasive atmosphere of devotion.

I was anxious to discover where it was Edith had spent so much prayer time with Our Lady before her? Surely not, as I had always understood, by a picture of Our Lady of Sorrows - which I could not find - but by the Pietà in the Lady Chapel? This is made of linden wood, approximately two-foot high and came from the Swabian school dating back to 1430–1450. It is a striking statue. Our Lady is seated with her dead Lord lying across her lap and held with the utmost tenderness. Her suffering face is poignant and it is easy to see why Edith and many others are drawn here to pray. I did so briefly, bringing to mind Edith's upright kneeling figure, in silent contemplation, not for thirty minutes or an hour but for two, three or more hours.

As we prepared to leave we saw two of the Benedictine brothers undertaking their evening tasks. One was in his carpet slippers carrying a watering can to top up the flower vases, while the other was renewing the sanctuary lamp. Edith Milleder asked: was there anything else I wanted to see? Was it possible, I enquired, to visit the crypt where Abbot Raphael was buried? The sacristan immediately fetched the key and took us below. The Abbot was one of Edith's most trusted and intimate friends and I had always been attracted by his strong, discerning gaze. It troubled me to think he may not have been entirely happy about the status of his community and beautiful Abbey during the war years, whilst he was far away in Algiers. I said a prayer for him as I made a mental note of his death in 1966. Edith kept in touch with Abbot Raphael while in Echt Carmel and in a letter written to Mother Petra Brüning in April 1939 she says: 'With V.E.R. [Walzer] I now have easy and speedy connections, and need no longer go on a detour through B. [Beuron] or Rome. Judging by his brief greetings, he is at peace and is satisfied, lives as a simple monk, makes himself useful wherever he can, and therefore has a lot of work.' In the days of censorship Edith considered it wise to use only initials when referring to the Abbot or Beuron.

As we climbed the steps out of the crypt, I realized this day of days must end. Pilgrimages take many different routes for different reasons. Mine may be considered unusual, even eccentric, with pony-judging the main focus of the German visit. The reality was: if there had been no pony-judging, there would have been no expenses-paid visit and no good friends like Edith and Beatrice. During eight days in Germany I brushed shoulders with the German culture and with three major cities. I travelled many road miles and savoured a glimpse of Edith Stein's world. As we drove away from Beuron, for the very first time I became aware of the vastness of 'her' world and the contrasts it compassed. I had only touched the tip of Edith's plenteous life.

On my return from South Africa later in the same year (see chapter four), I had to spend several days as a convalescent. The doctor believed the cold I suffered in such adverse conditions in Germany had been partly responsible for my illness in Lesotho. It was time to take a break in order to recover fully. I welcomed the opportunity to reflect on so many things. The South African and German experience, the uncertainty about the future of the Presteigne community, my own failings during my time at Carmel, the prospect of my mother's move to Herefordshire, and gratitude for all the joys as well as the sorrows of the past three years. I often asked myself whether I had made a mistake believing I could retain so much of my old life while setting out on a new one. At times, it seemed, this might have been the case; but at others I reasoned that without the old I would hardly have survived the new. Perhaps, after all, this was God's plan for me. Whatever the future might hold, the past must never be a cause for regret. Tomorrow was another day.

CHAPTER SIX

Decision Time

I was determined to face in positive mode what was likely to be a difficult year in 1988 and so I began work on a sequel to *Shrouded in Mist*. The increasing popularity of the Connemara pony overseas was evident with the birth of breed societies not only in Europe and the USA but also in Australia, New Zealand and South Africa. *Shrouded in Mist* had been well received and I was encouraged to write a sequel. An overview of the breed, around the world, was likely to be a vast undertaking. In my capacity as an international judge I had visited many countries and hoped that I was equal to providing a worthwhile study. I was soon working my way through stud books, old diaries, show catalogues and memories. *Out of the Mist* was an absorbing task.

At the same time, the younger of my two ponies was suffering from lung damage and it did not respond to treatment. Gazelle held a special place in my heart and the decision to send her to greener pastures was an agonizing one to take. For some time my neighbour had been considering whether or not he would sell me two acres of land (I bought Combe Cottage with a little less than two acres). A further two would provide a home for two or three ponies, should the day come when I no longer had the use of land at Carmel. It was a wise investment and the contract was signed on 25 March.

Meanwhile, life at Carmel moved on. A chalet had been built to accommodate a Benedictine sister, Scholastica, who was living the eremitical life. She was formally received into the Diocese of Menevia, as a hermit, in mid-February. Sister Joan and I began the task of cataloguing the guesthouse library. Susan and Chris came regularly once a month on a Sunday afternoon for formation with Sister Paddy. We often shared tea and a gossip at Combe Cottage afterwards. I drove Sister Anne to various appointments for discussions concerning the future of the community.

Teresa Elwes visited in order to work on the inscription designed for the east wall of the chapel by David Jones, the one rejected by the community in the 1950s. For three or four days Teresa 'took over' the guests' dining room and my well-ordered life. Like many artists she was unconventional and untidy and was determined to mix her noxious paints in my kitchen sink. She was, at the same time, an engaging character who took immense care to paint the inscription as prescribed. It was a special moment in the life of the chapel when it was eventually mounted on 15 March.

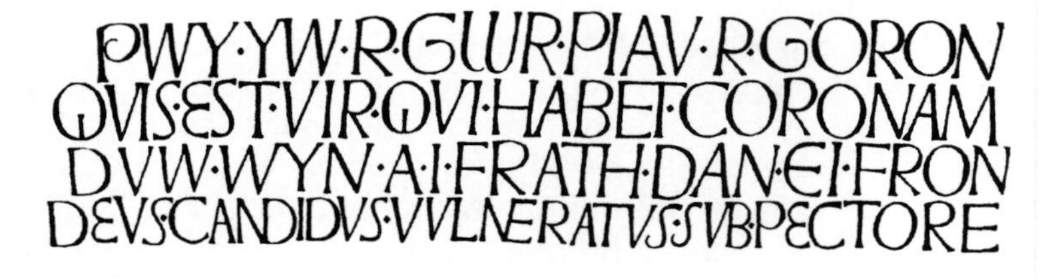

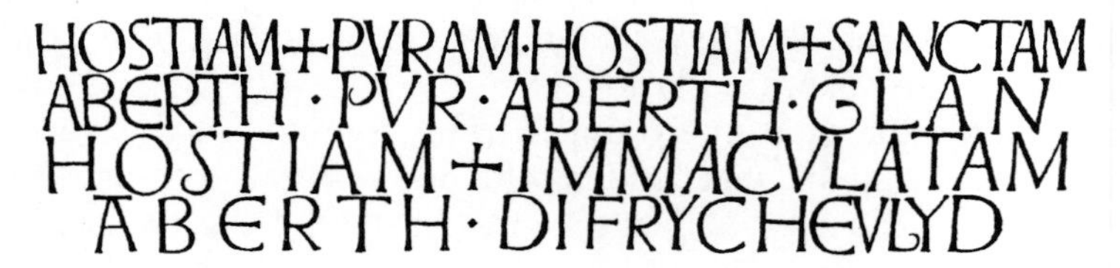

Who is the man who owns the crown?
The White God with the wound under his heart.
A pure sacrifice, a holy sacrifice,
An undefiled sacrifice.

Inscription, by David Jones, for the east wall of the chapel, Presteigne Carmel. (The original can be seen in the National Library of Wales.)

On Ash Wednesday I was told Sisters Joan and Rosalie were probably going to South Africa for a year. The following day I took them to a local photographer for passport photos. I never did understand where this proposition was likely to lead us.

Abbot John made his spring visit on 18 March. It was so good to see him. Father Ted Yarnold, SJ arrived on the twenty-fifth of the same month in order to make his retreat before celebrating the Easter liturgy with the community and the parish.

On 12 April Abbot Jerome, the Ecclesiastical Superior and Abbot of Belmont Abbey, visited. The air was full of tension and it was obvious something momentous was afoot. On 14 April the decision to close the Carmel was voted on and taken. I, like everybody else, was in a daze. What would become of us all, I wondered? On 21 April I took Sisters Joan and Rosalie to Shrewsbury hospital for yellow fever injections. They were now talking about a three-month visit to South Africa instead of a year.

I was grateful that two of my oldest friends were arriving to stay at Combe Cottage for three nights. Spending time with them brought some signs of normality back to life. We visited the Cambrian tweed factory and went out for an evening meal. I was sorry to see them leave.

As was often the case during my time at Carmel, I found it distressing that 'discretion' blurred the reality and the fact of closure was only released piecemeal. Two of the sisters shared their ideas for the future with me. Sister Clare decided not to move to another Carmel but hoped to embrace the life of a hermit, preferably somewhere in Wales. Sister Paddy was considering her position. She had good friends in Wood Hall Carmel in Yorkshire but might a return to Ireland be a better idea, she wondered. The greatest concern was for the future of the two eldest, Sister Monica in her eighties and Sister Flora who had just celebrated her seventy-fifth birthday.

On 27 April I hitched the pony trailer to the car and drove to Hampshire. My mother's move to Leominster was finally arranged. I was to help with the last of the packing up and bring everything, except the main items of furniture, in the pony trailer. I could not help being sad that my mother was leaving Barton-on-Sea, an area she loved so well. She was now in her eighties and realized it was prudent to live nearer to my sister and myself. She had twelve years in Leominster but, sadly, was never very happy there.

I celebrated the first anniversary of Edith's beatification on 1 May, quietly and on my own. The new boundary fence was erected at Combe Cottage. The Cistercian sisters from Stapehill expressed an interest in the Presteigne monastery, as they searched for smaller premises. The news of dispersal was made public officially on 2 May. Sister Mary went to Sclerder for a preliminary visit and various members from the Stapehill community visited in ones and twos. On 6 May, I went to Boars Hill for the weekend with Father John Hughes and Edith Stein. I was in need of Edith's support now more than ever and was grateful for the opportunity to become closer to her in these three days.

I returned home with Volume 2 in the ICS series of The Collected Works of Edith Stein: *Essays on Woman*, edited by Dr Lucy Gelber and Romaeus Leuven, OCD and translated by Freda Oben, Ph.D. I did not find this an easy read. To be a member of the audience when Edith delivered her lectures would, I believe, have assisted me in a better understanding of her profound messages. As it was, I had to be content with an occasional passage that I found relevant to my own life.

The translator, Freda Oben, is an American mother of five, a Jewess who converted to Catholicism and who, when introduced to Edith Stein, determined to read her works in the original. This involved learning German. No small task to do so and then to translate what she read in German back into English. *Essays on Woman* was published in 1987. The following year Alba House in the USA published *Edith Stein: Scholar, Feminist, Saint* by Freda Oben. It is a small work of three chapters.

In 2001, the same publishers provided an interesting further work by Oben, *The Life and Thought of St. Edith Stein*. This is a lively and thought-provoking portrait of Edith, with which I found myself largely in tune. The following quotation (from her first work) indicates how close to Edith she became as she read *Life in a Jewish Family*. She writes: '[Edith] loved nature and took frequent hikes and picnics with her friends. I followed her route to Nikolausberg almost expecting to come upon the "three wind-stripped trees" which had reminded her of Golgotha – a strange image to come to the mind of this young Jewish atheist!' This echoed my own thoughts precisely.

It was on my return from Oxford that I decided to consign *Out of the Mist* to another day and cancelled my pre-arranged August holiday in Connemara. I realized it would be impractical for me to be away for any length of time while so much was happening at Carmel.

Susan, Chris and I welcomed Paddy's decision to go to Wood Hall. We would be able to keep in touch with her there. She was taking Sister Monica with her, the best possible arrangement for Monica. After consultation with a map and the *Diocesan Year Book,* Sister Clare decided to explore Aberystwyth, where the parish was in the care of the O Carm Fathers of Aylesford. An appointment was made to meet the parish priest, Father Hugh Clarke, on 18 May and subject to his approval, to look for a suitable hermitage. I feared this would be like looking for a needle in a haystack. Sister Clare, on the other hand, did not foresee any problems. We set off on a bright and sunny morning and met Father Hugh after the 9.30 a.m. Mass. He was positive, kind and welcoming.

We bought the local newspaper and visited the estate agents in the town. Two things were apparent. Means were limited and privacy important. Sister Clare's faith that God would provide was fully justified. A short walk from the Carmelite church, on a hill overlooking the bay, were two Victorian houses split into holiday flats. They were being sold flat by flat. A small one in the middle of Ael-y-Don, and fully furnished, was within our means. The estate agent pointed out it might not be as quiet as Clare would wish if students occupied the flats above or below, but this did not deter her. We returned to Aberystwyth the following day with Sister Anne who approved of the flat and the purchase was set in motion. I could hardly believe we had crossed such a big hurdle with so much ease.

Amidst all the plans for closure, the community were set to celebrate the Golden Jubilee of the Carmel's foundation on 1 July. Founded from Notting Hill Carmel in 1938 it was first situated in Watford. In 1942 the community moved to Berkhamstead, and in 1951 to Presteigne. It seemed hardly possible that a celebration could take place, when so soon there would no longer be a community. Nonetheless it was agreed, with great courage, to observe the occasion in a fitting manner and invitations were sent to friends old and new. In reality it provided an excellent opportunity for many friends to say goodbye to the sisters on a happy occasion. But for some of us, the day was too full of pathos for comfort.

The preparations for 1 July appeared to give Sister Anne a focus while still in a state of shock. We spent time together in the parlour to make plans. It was apparent that the number of guests expected would exceed the capacity of the guesthouse. I suggested a marquee be erected between the sacristy and guesthouse. The large parlour would open onto this and allow the sisters to meet their guests in comfort in twos and threes or more at a time. Additional crockery, cutlery and the like, would be required. Friends could be asked to assist in the provision of a buffet lunch. The sisters' choir, if opened, would provide space for the overspill from the laity's side of the chapel. It was going to be a big undertaking with the bulk of the responsibility on my shoulders. At least it provided something positive to occupy my mind and my energy.

In order to celebrate the Golden Jubilee in a fitting manner, the David Jones inscription had already been commissioned and mounted. And Jane Quail had been asked to undertake a carving on the stone roundel above the main door. It depicts the Assumption with Our Lady shown as the 'woman clothed with the sun' (Rev. 12:1). Jane's husband Paul designed and made two stained-glass windows for either side of the tabernacle, the rising of the sun to the east and its setting to the west. The Quails stayed in the guesthouse while doing their work and were delightful people to entertain. These additions to the chapel complemented the building without disturbing its simple charm.

Once the Presteigne sisters were accepted by the Carmels of their choice, the prioress of the Carmel in question visited Presteigne to select items that might be useful to them. The altar-bread machine was earmarked for Sclerder Carmel and so on. There was a constant flow of visitors and trains to be met. Sisters Vivien and Flora went by train to Glasgow in order to visit Dumbarton Carmel. It was a disruptive and painful period through which we had to work and pray our way.

On 5 June I began a five-day retreat in preparation for my Definitive Promise on 10 June, the feast of the Sacred Heart. The community had a small hermitage, which had taken the place of the caravan, where they spent their quiet days. Formerly the dairy, it was situated beside the old cow shed which I used for lambing. I asked if I could I use it – The Cenacle, as it was known – during my days of retreat. I could not help feeling hurt when the request was refused without any reason being given. Paddy prepared a programme for me for the five days using the theme of *Gift*. When I knew I was unable to use The Cenacle I decided to go to Combe Cottage each morning after Mass, returning in time for Vespers and my period of preparation with Paddy. It was a peaceful grace-filled time spent with the Lord.

Abbot John arrived on the morning of the tenth and I was able to meet and talk with him. By a strange coincidence he gave me a penance (after confession) that I had to search for in my old Roman Missal. I spent an hour with it, in chapel, before the ceremony. Memories of my schooldays and the teaching sisters to whom I owed so much were vivid. The Missal was their gift when I was received into the Church and now it lived unused and unloved on a shelf in my bookcase. I am glad I had need of it on this special day.

Sister Rosalie kindly prepared an order of service for Vespers and on the cover was Edith in her habit with a quotation from her poem *Holy Night* beneath: 'A star rose before me, gentle and clear. Steadily it guided me – and I followed'. Sister Flora made me a large scapular from the material used for the sisters' Carmelite habits. Abbot John prepared a short sermon that I have kept and treasured. He had a dreadful back-to-front handwriting that was always difficult to decipher but the text was invariably short and pithy. He spoke of my commitment as a silent way, no obvious heroics, a way of prayer and a way of love, pondering in your heart the mystery of God. I did not experience the great joy I had anticipated. There was too much sadness in the house. But there was peace in my heart, and whatever the future might hold, I felt secure as a dedicated member of the Carmelite family.

Susan, Chris and Jo were there to share the occasion and prepared a lovely evening meal to follow the ceremony. Abbot John and Father Peter, the chaplain, joined the four of us.

On 13 June, a sister from South Africa, a member of the Order of the White Sisters, came to share her knowledge of South Africa with the community and stayed for three nights. She was a lovely person who inspired us all. I was aware she had grave reservations about the very unclear ideas some members of our community had in relation to the life of a contemplative in Africa. One sister believed the South African idea was always a red herring and I could see it was muddying the waters of closure.

1 July was a bright, clear day. Susan and Chris arrived with cakes and trifles, my friends John and Susan Bowen with flowers for the chapel and boiled eggs for the salad, and so on. It was not easy to keep a clear head and to ensure everything ran smoothly. Mass was scheduled for midday and the clergy arrived in good time for a concelebrated Mass. The tiny sanctuary could hardly accommodate them all. There were three bishops and three abbots and as far I can remember four further priests. Sister Vivien made ten white chasubles for the occasion, so all were robed in identical fashion. The small chapel was packed. A buffet lunch in the marquee was enjoyed by everyone and it was late afternoon before the last guest had departed. By that time I was physically and emotionally spent. I sobbed myself to sleep that night.

I suffered reaction to this big day and found myself at odds with community plans when I was told they preferred to travel by train than by car on their various excursions. I felt redundant and wondered why I had given up my Irish holiday. It was quite wrong of me to feel this way, and there were countless small runs to be made to dentist, optician and hearing clinics. It was important each sister moved to her new home with her health checked out.

On 9 July Susan Revill made her First Promise as a secular Carmelite at Vespers. It was only a small celebration but a happy one, especially for Paddy and myself. It ensured that Susan's commitment would be carried forward, in spite of the imminent closure of the Carmel.

On the feast of Our Lady of Mount Carmel we hosted a wine and cheese party for members of the parish, those who had not been with us on 1 July, and for the many friends the sisters had made in the locality over the years. It was another farewell. Forty or more were present. It was a sunny evening and we were able to gather in the courtyard outside the parlour, as on 1 July, before joining the community for Compline at 8.45 p.m. Peter and I found ourselves washing up, talking and drinking wine until 12.30 a.m.

Now that my mother was living nearby, there were extra family gatherings, mostly at the weekend. She was very understanding of my commitments to Carmel and undemanding. I was grateful for this.

At the very last moment Sister Anne decided to visit Langham Carmel, a long drive to the east. I was 'needed' unexpectedly. Sister Bernadette came with us. Was Sister Anne considering this as a future home for herself? Paul and Jane Quail lived not far from Langham and I was invited to spend the day with them. We had a picnic on the beach and I relaxed. The prioress of Langham returned to Presteigne with us three days later.

Notes in my diary for this time tell me two sisters from Dumbarton visited and that Sister Flora finally accepted an invitation to join their community. Sister Vivien had already done so. Sisters Rosalie and Joan received work permits for their visit to South Africa. Sister Rosalie left on 2 August. I drove her to Heathrow Airport and Sister Anne came with us. On 8 August I took Sister Joan to Newport station. She was on her way to join Sister Rosalie at Wynberg, the Cape Town Carmel in South Africa. Two weeks later they were both on their way to Nairobi Carmel. The visit to Wynberg was a disappointment and unlikely to be beneficial. They returned to Presteigne on 17 September. Prior to leaving the UK Joan and Rosalie had visited Ireland. Malahide Carmel, Dublin was ready to receive them as members of their community on their return from South Africa.

On Edith Stein's feast, 9 August, I drove Paddy and Monica to Wood Hall in Yorkshire. The day before I bought a lovely mauve gloxinia for the chapel in Edith's honour. Vivien invited me to compose a closing prayer for the offices on her feast. The Church had not yet done so. A large statue of Our Lady from the ante-choir was to travel with us to Yorkshire. I tied 'her' into a rear seat with binder twine and Monica sat beside her. We had some strange looks from those travelling behind us! Monica collected her few personal belongings into a yellow bucket. This was placed outside her cell with a note requesting it be kept upright during the journey. This was typical Monica. Resourceful and practical, to the end. I loaded the car in front of the house and those of us who were left shared an ice cream 'farewell' with Paddy and Monica. The departures got more and more sad.

As we drove north, Paddy reminisced about her journey to Presteigne from Edinburgh Carmel twenty years earlier. She had hoped and expected it would be her last move. Monica spoke hardly at all. She kept her thoughts and her memories to herself. I had packed a picnic lunch that we shared at a halfway point. We arrived at Wood Hall in time for Vespers. The following morning I made friends with two of the community and said goodbye to Paddy and Monica. Paddy was to return to Presteigne to help with packing up, once Monica was settled. I had a long, lonely drive home.

Jo and I had planned a weekend on the Lleyn Peninsula where kind friends lent us their house. After the stress of the last weeks it was a welcome break with lovely walks along the beach and headland, morning lie-ins and good reading. I returned in time to take Sister Clare to her new home.

It was 31 August; I drove the car, with the trailer attached, to the front of the house. A local firm, Wells Fargo, had lorries for hire and transported just about anything. We hired them regularly throughout the dispersal. One of their smaller vans came to complement my trailer for the removal of Clare's belongings to Aberystwyth. These were simple enough: a chair, a desk and work table, her small printing press as well as her typewriter, books, a small harp and boxes of print. And of course bedding, cooking utensils and everything needed for daily life. It seemed only yesterday that I had collected the entire Belmont printing press and transported it to Presteigne. Now part of it was on the move again. Somehow Clare's departure was symbolic, the end of an era. She had been a Presteigne foundation sister, in the novitiate with Sister Anne, one of the builders of the chapel, and at different times prioress and novice mistress. Clare was a leader in choir and always present on time. I knew Anne felt her going deeply. Clare herself was composed and ready for her new life.

Anne came with us to Aberystwyth and fixed some shelves in the flat for Clare, while we unpacked the vehicles. Because the flat was on the second floor it was in every way an uphill task and one wondered where Clare would sit or sleep when we left her. To say the flat was overfull was an understatement.

On the feast of the Exaltation of the Cross, there were only four of us in choir for Vespers: Paddy, Flora, Vivien and myself. Anne and Bernadette were away in London. At this very time the Pope was in Lesotho to beatify an Oblate missionary, Father Joseph Gerard. I could well imagine the joy and celebrations in Lesotho and was with them in prayer and in spirit. A very happy letter arrived from Clare. She had no phone at this stage. On 17 September Joan and Rosalie arrived home from Nairobi.

On 25 September I was aware it was four years to the day since I had arrived at Carmel. It seemed more like forty. A few lines written in my diary at this time remind me how it was: 'I cannot make the move to get to bed these nights and then cannot wake up or get up next morning.' On the feast of Our Lady of Sorrows I picked up the 1988 Spring edition of *Mount Carmel* for my breakfast reading and found an article, 'Standing with you beneath the Cross: Blessed Edith Stein's devotion to Mary'. As always, Edith appeared at my side in my hour of need.

Ireland was the next stop. I hired a small trailer for this journey into which we packed the artefacts and personal belongings of Joan and Rosalie. We left home at 7.00 a.m. and, after a delayed journey from Holyhead, arrived at Dun Laoghaire at 7.30 p.m. The Malahide sisters provided a hot meal for the four of us in the parlour. How kind of them not to leave me on my own after the long journey, as was the usual practice when I delivered sisters to Carmel. I spent the night in a local bed and breakfast, the owners of which became, and still are, my very good friends. The following day I met my pony friend, Donal Kenny, in The Grand Hotel where we shared Lesotho and pony news. Anne and I returned to England two days later, calling for tea with Clare at Aberystwyth on the way. It all sounds very matter of fact. But it was a further break-up of the family, full of 'contained' emotion – apart, that is, from a few tears shed by Rosalie, as we crossed the Irish Sea and the Welsh mountains dissolved in the distance.

On 16 October, I drove Vivien and Flora to Dumbarton

with Flora sitting in the front seat beside me. I knew the inner agony this dear old sister was suffering. There was so much of Flora in Presteigne. When her precious livestock were dispersed, the greenhouse and the growing of grapes and tomatoes had taken their place. The border alongside was filled with colourful dahlias and Flora's hands were evidence of this work that she undertook with such joy and diligence. The same rough hands were skilled with the needle and as 'robe mistress' she filled her final weeks at Presteigne making new habits for each member of the community who required one. There was no doubt in my mind about the warmth of welcome our sisters received at Dumbarton. But for Sister Flora the change of culture and environment, the Scottish accent (to someone with poor hearing) and a house on so many different levels (that presented difficulties to her unsteady feet) were all part of a difficult adjustment. She faced up to it gallantly and spent nearly four years in Scotland before dying, unexpectedly, in July 1992.

A quotation from my diary reads: 'Vivien has worked hard to leave everything straight behind her. Because she and Flora have been so faithful to the office, and each to their daily tasks, it seemed as if they would be here forever. Now they are going and it really begins to look like the end.' As Anne and I drove away from Dumbarton forty-eight hours later, it felt just like that. We made a long detour on the way home in order to visit Assumpta at Hawick. It was a timely visit, for ten days later she died.

On the feast of St Teresa of Avila, Susan and Chris came for the day. Anne and Paddy were the only sisters in the Carmel. I cooked a special vegetarian lunch and passed portions 'inside' to them. Under all the circumstances I wonder why the five of us did not share the meal? The following day I took Anne to the station on her way to Hawick. Assumpta was said to be in heart failure. I was asked to stay in the Carmel to keep Paddy company while Anne was away. How quickly things can change! It was no longer possible or practical to observe 'enclosure' but it required an emergency for this to happen. Enclosure had caused me so much pain in the last four years and it seemed I was to remain at the other end of a bell, even though to all intents and purposes the Carmel was now closed. Dear old Assumpta, in her sickness, proved the catalyst. It was decided she should be buried in her much-loved home town of Chorley, and on 20 October I drove Anne and Paddy there for her Requiem Mass.

Bernadette remained very uncertain about her future and came and went, using Presteigne as her base. On 22 November, I had to return Paddy to Wood Hall. I knew how much Anne and I would miss her. It was arranged that Vivien would take her place for a short visit in order to bring the accounts up to date. After dropping Paddy off, I met Vivien at Leeds station and we drove back to Presteigne together. She sounded so happy and settled at Dumbarton and had good news of Flora. By this time I was sharing meals with the sisters and doing a full share of helping with packing up and clearing out. It was a soul-destroying task walking round the cold, empty cloisters, workrooms and cells. Only the kitchen was warm. Worse than the cold was sorting through all that had been part of 'life' in Carmel and deciding where best this or that might be needed or useful.

While all this was going on, Anne was chasing shadows in her attempt to find possible purchasers for the property. The Cistercian sisters had long since decided against its suitability, and while Knight, Frank and Rutley were the official estate agents, Anne seemed inclined to follow her own agenda. A lay group from London expressed interest and made repeated visits and stop-overs. A local health care team were invited to explore the possibility of a nursing home. Another faction was asked to consider it as a retirement home for elderly contemplatives. The land was on offer for development to a local husband and wife. They had design ideas but no cash. Time and energy were wasted on fruitless, unrealistic visions.

The chapel was attached to the main house through the ante-choir, and the extern quarters through the turn. These two buildings had to be detached from the house by constructing interior walls at the relevant dividing lines. On 18 November I was told the chapel, complete with choir and sacristy, was to be given to the Diocese. No decision was taken on the extern quarters, the priest's bungalow or the hermit's chalet. The future of the four acres remained 'on hold' but the house with the lovely walled garden, cow shed and ancillary buildings, could now be sold separately.

The house, a Grade II listed building, is not unattractive,

but the attachment of a line of sleeper-built cells, a flat-roofed large community room and a flat-roofed infirmary wing of four bedrooms, together with the close proximity of chapel and cottage, detracted from the general appeal of the property. Knight, Frank and Rutley became involved again.

Piece by piece I had been slowly moving my own possessions to Combe Cottage. They sat in the middle of the rooms in an untidy pile. I had never attempted to make the cottage feel like home. Now I had to do just that and had little inspiration or inclination for the task. I asked a builder to put up some bookshelves and an electrician to install two night storage heaters. This was as far as I got. Christmas was on the horizon. Anne was going away, I cannot remember where to, and friends of hers were coming to take care of the property. My cottage at Carmel, no longer Mynydd but now Ty Mair, had to be made ready and welcoming for the caretakers, a family of four. It was finally time for me to move out. I spent Christmas with my family but it is a distant blur. 1988 had been such a turbulent year. I was not sorry to see it end.

The Presteigne sisters 'at work'. Sister Anne wheels the barrow, watched by (from L to R) Sister Margaret, Mother Michael and Sister Magdalen of Jesus (Charlotte Spitz).

Presteigne Carmel, the sisters' choir stalls behind the new sliding grille.

A sketch of the Carmelite chapel, drawn by Father Nicholas Madden, OCD in 1987.

Donald Nicholl, taken a few months before his death in May 1997.

Abbot John Roberts, OSB. Abbot of Downside 1974–1990.

The circular tower of the Chapel of Atonement, Dachau.

Sister Amata Neyer, OCD in the parlour at Cologne Carmel, 1987.

The Pietà in the Abbey of Beuron.

Left: Sister Flora of Jesus (Hilda Violet Holmes 1913–1992). A Carmelite for 52 years.

Sister Monica of Jesus (Monica Selby Hall 1902–1992). A Carmelite for 66 years.

Sister Mary Assumpta (Nellie Hart 1900–1988). A Carmelite for 46 years.

Presteigne Carmel, the exterior of the sisters' choir (now the annexe) with a new entrance.

The extern quarters. (The writer's bedroom was above the porch, to the right, with the two small windows.)

Jane Quail engraving the roundel in 1988.

Father Nicholas Madden, OCD in 2003.

Sister Josephine Koeppel, OCD in the Edith Stein archive room, Cologne Carmel, 1994.

Dr Joanne Mosley delivers a lecture on the life and work of Edith Stein, 'Avila', Dublin, 2001.

A memento from the Mass celebrating the centenary of the birth of Edith Stein, at Cologne Carmel, 12 October 1991.

A prayer card celebrating the canonization, 11 October 1998, depicting the Reno painting.

Sue Revill and Chris Hemson share a celebration with Sister Paddy in 1988.

Secular Carmelites Janet, Eddie and Judy with Father Matt, in the Presteigne Church in 1996. Note the David Jones Chi Rho on the wall behind them. (The original is on permanent loan to the National Library of Wales, Aberystwyth, for conservation.)

Father Emmanuel McCarthy's icon of Edith Stein, Sister Teresia Benedicta of the Cross.

The offertory procession at Mass on the day of Edith Stein's canonization, Sunday 11 October 1998.

Father John Sullivan, OCD at the OCDS International Conference in Rome, 1996.

Father Matt Blake, OCD in Rome, 1998.

Father Michael Linssen, OCD and Dr Lucy Gelber, 1997.

The grave of Sister Magdalen in the Carmelite cemetery, Presteigne. The inscription reads: 'Sr. Magdalen of Jesus (Charlotte Spitz) Aged 66 Professed 17.1.1947 Died 5.5.1960.

The Carmelite cemetery, Presteigne.

CHAPTER SEVEN

Betwixt and Between

Susan and I were invited to celebrate the New Year (1989) with Chris and her husband Tony at their cottage, White Castle, which overlooks the ancient Dore Abbey in the heart of the Golden Valley. Tony accompanied us on the piano as we sang hymns at Vespers and Compline and then Auld Lang Syne to see the New Year in. What better way to begin another year, one that appeared to be full of uncertainties and question marks.

I returned to Combe Cottage and the task of making it feel like home. I transformed the smaller of the two guest bedrooms into a small oratory. Because I had become accustomed to sharing the daily office with the community in chapel, I realized I would require a new focus, a discipline, to ensure a regular pattern for private, solitary prayer in the future. On the eve of the Epiphany I lit a candle and welcomed the Three Kings as I said evening prayer for the first time in my own small oratory.

Carmel was now considered closed but two or three sisters remained, and came and went as the occasion demanded (Vivien and Paddy did a repeat shuttle service in the New Year), all the time continuing with the task of clearing the monastery. I shared Mass with them most mornings and was ready to help whenever needed and remained the 'on demand' chauffeur. At various times visits to the Bishop, the solicitor and the estate agent were necessary. By Easter the remaining sisters had moved from the main house into Ty Mair, although the building was not yet totally clear. Great care was taken to send everything to where it was likely to be most needed and appreciated. Towards the end, the hospice shop in Hereford and a bonfire were the main recipients.

The future of the house and ancillary buildings was not yet resolved, but plans were drawn for the reordering of the chapel with its future use as a parish church in mind. The sisters' choir was made accessible from the drive rather than through the ante-choir as hitherto. A small porch was built at the entrance to it. The grille was replaced by a sliding screen so that the extra space provided by the choir could be used, or not, as required. The choir area (now known as the annexe) has since often served a dual purpose being used for exhibitions, meetings, coffee mornings and sales of work. The altar rails on the laity's side of the chapel were removed. A new boundary behind the priest's house and hermit chalet was drawn and another beyond the cow shed. At last the future of the property began to look a little clearer.

On 18 March I drove Paddy back to Wood Hall for the last time. It was just one more goodbye but, oh so hard. It was Palm Sunday next day and Susan and Chris came over to spend the evening with me. They were experiencing the same feeling of loss, and to share this was a comfort to the three of us.

On 20 March Anne told me she had decided to go to Rivonia Carmel in South Africa. The Bishop had insisted on a decision even though he knew she was not yet ready to leave Presteigne. She would be joining Bernadette who had already been accepted by Rivonia Carmel.

The chaplain and parish priest, Father Peter, had been a good friend and support throughout the last four years. He was a comparatively young man and enjoyed giving me a hand with the livestock from time to time. We often shared a meal and a glass of wine at the end of the day. The twin parish of Presteigne and Knighton was small in numbers but presented its own particular problems. Peter believed he would be better situated living in Knighton and once the monastery closed he was free to move. A house was bought and in April I moved all his furniture in my pony trailer. The house was not in an ideal position, and in time, it proved to be an unwise move. Worse still, shortly after Peter had settled in Knighton, he learnt he was to be transferred to the Diocese of Wrexham and would be leaving early in July. I was losing yet another good friend.

Abbot John continued to make his quarterly visits and these were welcomed by us all. He stayed at Combe Cottage and said Mass for us and listened sympathetically to our various concerns. I don't know what we would have done without his listening ear and sound advice.

On 1 May I turned to Edith as had become my habit. She was never far away but special days with her were occasions of renewal, of asking for courage, and of knowing that however many friends I might lose during this period of change she, at least, would always be there for me. My trust in her had become implicit.

Life was very full, and I overstretched myself in order to draw a veil over the undercurrent of change and loss. *Out of the Mist* was taking a good slice of my time most days. The grass in the garth and prayer garden at Presteigne required regular mowing. My own very small garden at Combe was in need of a new look. The hours in the garden were therapeutic and restored me when my mind became clogged with pedigrees and pony family trees.

Chiltern Cameo produced a bonny colt foal on 5 May and I felt free to spend a week in Connemara by the middle of the month. I had not returned to the West of Ireland since 1984. I knew I would find refreshment of mind and body once I reached Clifden. I stayed for a mere week, in the misguided belief that the sisters who remained in Presteigne could not manage without me. I was lent the Errislannan Gate Lodge in which I had spent three months in 1981 while working on *Shrouded in Mist*. It was like coming home.

As I took long walks out to the sea along the Errislannan Peninsula, with a soft, moist west wind blowing on my cheeks, I thought of Edith who walked and trekked in the countryside when her brilliant mind became congealed and at a standstill; when she would have welcomed being run over by a bus. The hills and the forests above Göttingen were far removed from Ireland's western seaboard, but God's gift of beauty in the countryside is ever the same. I sat under the shade of a sycamore tree in the Gate Lodge garden as I worked on the New Zealand chapter for *Out of the Mist*. I recalled the lives of the forebears of the first Connemara ponies who were exported to the greener pastures of New Zealand. They had lived and worked on the Errislannan roads in the 1930s and 1940s and were the hardy originals of the breed. Errislannan Blackie was the great-great-grand-dam of the first stallion to arrive in New Zealand, Connemara Park Roy.

Shortly after my return to Presteigne the last vestiges of the enclosure wall were removed by a mechanical digger. The chapel bell was rehung and the rope to toll it took up its new position in the chapel, having formerly been conveniently placed in the ante-choir. Sister Joan returned from Ireland, not having been able to settle there. By now it had been decided to transfer the extern quarters, guesthouse, priest's bungalow and hermit chalet to the Diocese. In June, contracts were exchanged for the sale of the main house to a family in Presteigne. They ran a small cottage industry designing and making children's clothes and required additional space to extend the business.

On 24 June my mother's elder sister and my godmother, Auntie Mary, celebrated her ninetieth birthday. I drove my mother to Chichester for the celebrations where we had a great family reunion. On 7 July Peter said his last Mass in Presteigne and on the same day Susan, Chris and I drove to Yorkshire to spend two nights at Wood Hall, in order to have time with Paddy and to see how Monica was. On 21 July my great-niece Lara Lucy was born. This was a very welcome event, after a long wait by her parents for the gift of a child.

Towards the end of the month I undertook a marathon journey to the North with a heavily loaded pony trailer. It contained the grille and sundry desks and prayer stools. The grille – used to divide the sisters' choir from the laity – was comparatively new. It had been designed to replace the original heavy fixed grille. It was in wrought iron, lightweight, easy to see through and on wheels, so that it moved smoothly back and forth as desired. I delivered my load to Liverpool Carmel and from there I drove to Preston Carmel where I left the trailer for a few days before moving onto an overnight stay in a hotel prior to judging at the Royal Lancashire Show. From there I drove to Boarbank Hall for a brief visit to my Augustinian friends, returning home less than a week later.

On Edith Stein's feast, 9 August, I spent a hermit day at Combe Cottage but was almost too tired to pray. I simply rested in her company. On the twelfth I celebrated my sixtieth birthday and spent a happy day with Jo, the remaining sisters and Anne's Ursuline sister, Biddy, together with a member of her community, who were on holiday in Presteigne. A large picnic was packed in a laundry basket; two dogs, my Chloe and Biddy's Megan, and the human assembly crammed into two cars and made for a sunny spot beside the river Wye in sight of the handsome Bredwardine Bridge. We enjoyed the picnic while the dogs had fun and games in the river. Two days later I drove to Aberystwyth to spend Sister Clare's birthday with her.

Towards the end of August I left for three weeks in the USA. I was invited as guest speaker at the American Connemara Pony Society's AGM and to conduct a seminar the following day. This took place in New Hampshire and from there I travelled to Virginia, Ohio, Metamora and finally to San Francisco. On went my 'second hat' on this occasion as an acclaimed Connemara pony authority. So often I felt as if I was leading a double life, at no time more so than in the USA. I received a warm welcome from old friends, both human and equine, and confess that I half hoped this long spell away might finally break my ties with the sisters. In reality I was unlikely to 'sign off' while there was a Presteigne sister in need of my help – and I did not do so.

I joined Chris and Tony Hemson at Wood Hall for the feast of St Teresa on 15 October when Chris made her First Promise in the hands of Father Aidan, OSB. He was an old family friend living nearby in York and came across to Wood Hall to join the community for Vespers and to receive Chris formally. We three, Chris, Susan and I, never failed to appreciate the welcome we received from the Wood Hall sisters on so many occasions. They, together with Paddy, provided our Carmelite home which we lost with the closure of Presteigne.

On 14 September, I took Joan to the station to catch a train to Sclerder, the Carmel of her choice. And Anne, finally and lastly, on 13 December, to the Convent at Bartestree, near Hereford. But not before she had moved from Ty Mair to the hermit chalet and welcomed Barbara as caretaker. Barbara moved, plus all her books, into Ty Mair on 7 December. She ran a second-hand religious book service. It was not long before we discovered she was quite unsuitable as caretaker.

Abbot John paid his final visit on 11 December and said Mass for us in the chalet. He took the Presteigne archives to Downside for safe-keeping when he left. Anne's remaining possessions amounted to three bulging suitcases and the small desk at which she had done all her writing in the last months. These went with her to Bartestree. She remained in Herefordshire for some months in-between visits to Lisieux, to Dublin for a thirty-day retreat, the Priory at Boars Hill, and one or more English Carmels on different missions. I remained in close touch and ready to assist her in any way until she finally departed for South Africa on 25 June. One final occasion we shared remains clearly in my mind. Clare's sister, Pat Aston, died suddenly and unexpectedly. Anne realized how grave a loss this would be for Clare and so we drove to Wendover for the Requiem Mass. Following the funeral Clare returned to Presteigne with us before returning to Aberystwyth by train the following day. In God's Providence we were able to share her sorrow for twenty-four hours.

Some months passed before I became aware that I was not 'free' of my commitment to the Presteigne community, until 25 June 1990, when I said goodbye to Anne at Heathrow. A new life could not take root until I experienced a sense of 'freedom' from my service to the well-being of the community, of being 'available' if and when they needed me. It had been a consuming faithfulness, given in love. At last I had crossed the finishing line.

This litany of dates does not tell the whole story. A very young priest had been appointed in Peter's place. As long as there was a Carmelite presence in the parish, he felt unable to commission lay Eucharistic ministers or to form a parish council. I remember well his first act of independence. The sisters' choir stalls had been arranged as pews facing the altar. Father Ian took them to Knighton church and replaced them with the stacking chairs in use there. This change cut through me like a sword but he *was* the parish priest and it was *his* choice. Many more changes were set to follow and almost inevitably they were mostly painful ones for myself.

In my days as President of the Legion Curia we had met every quarter at the Gerrards Cross Carmelite Priory. My first

Carmelite friend was our spiritual director, Father Herman, OCD. He was a Cork man and a horseman and we immediately found we had much in common. In October 1988 he wrote the following on hearing that the Carmel was to close: 'I have just read your letter and realize what a trauma you must be going through – not unlike the Prioress at Compiègne seeing all the nuns through to the guillotine and having to hang back to the last herself. It is always unspeakably sad to see a house dedicated to the Lord passing into secular use, but then that is the stuff that so many of the old Irish poems are made of during the destruction of the monasteries. The important thing I suppose is that no matter where your abode is the altar of your heart remains unchanged.' He may have over-dramatized with his reference to Compiègne but it revealed his understanding of the loss I experienced as I said goodbye to each sister, the sadness at seeing the monastery gutted and the aloneness once the last sister had left. What he did not know was the length of time closure took and the added heartache this incurred.

As I reflect on the period of April 1988 through to December 1989, I realize how often I was able to relate to Edith's anguish on parting with her dearest mother and later her religious family of Cologne, only to be followed by the final goodbye at Echt. She endured each parting in God's hand and with great fortitude. In my own inadequate way I tried to do the same but I was not made of such stern stuff as she and regularly failed. One of her texts provided the inspiration and the help I sought. It was printed as a prayer card by the Carmelite sisters in Tasmania and its place on my desk is permanent. It reads: 'The Cross serves as a walking stick to speed one's march to the summit.' So often when I found myself unable to grasp the Cross, I used Edith as a walking stick.

CHAPTER EIGHT

Thank You Edith

The challenge of adapting to life without Carmel proved to be as great as it had been to live with it. It was impossible to wipe the slate clean while I continued to live in Presteigne, to be a member of the parish and to use the monastery land for my livestock. The problems the parish faced were huge and many a time I was not as supportive as I might have been. Parishioners experienced ten years of ups and downs interspersed with sad events. These times could fill a book but do not belong in this memoir and I am pleased to leave the book unopened.

I spent Easter 1990 at the Carmelite Priory, Oxford and some of my inner wounds healed. I went to Connemara in the spring and again in August. I was invited to judge in Germany for the second time and had various judging engagements up and down the country at home. From time to time I undertook 'babysitting' for my niece Nicola and came to know Lara Lucy.

A sense of 'loss' continued to pursue me throughout the year. In July I had to say goodbye to Arctic Moon. She was the three-year-old pony I bought in Connemara in 1964, who had founded my Chiltern stud, bred me sixteen foals and been an important part of my life for twenty-six years. In December her granddaughter, Chiltern Cameo, who was only fifteen years old, had to join her. Both ponies gave me endless success and pleasure as a breeder, and their absence from my home paddocks left a dull ache in my heart.

I remember 9 July as if it were yesterday. The vet arrived and I walked across the field to catch Moon, knowing what I had to do. She lifted her head with ears pricked as I approached her and moved across the field beside me in what had become her 'rickety' way with her head held high displaying her usual queenly pride. She went to greener pastures with her dignity intact and not as a worn-out old pony. Only Moon could have done so at the age of twenty-nine.

Writing about Connemara ponies, though they were not my own, was a form of memorial to the breed, to which my ponies belonged. I found my work at this time, on *Out of the Mist*, a constant source of consolation. When I read in Graham Greene's obituary that he believed 'to write is to keep one's sanity', I was inclined to agree with him.

Roger Whittaker, my brother-in-law, died in October, suddenly and unexpectedly, shortly after his retirement. A man of integrity, who had farmed most of his life, he was a good friend who often helped me with the livestock and I missed him.

In March I drove Abbot John to Wood Hall to see Paddy and Monica. It was a great reunion. We stayed there overnight and Father John spent a further two nights at Combe Cottage. On 7 July I drove to Wood Hall again in order to meet Abbot John and Susan Revill. Paddy had arranged for Susan to make her Final Promise as a secular Carmelite. Circumstances had delayed this event unduly. It represented another notable milestone in the life of our small secular family.

The Benedictine community of Downside held elections in December. Father John was not re-elected abbot. After sixteen years' service I believe he was more than ready to hand over the responsibility to someone else. In fact, he rather enjoyed acting as parish priest in an adjoining Downside parish. 'H' for humility was the master word throughout Father John's life. As long as he was able to drive, he continued to pay regular visits to Combe. When he had to give up his car, I occasionally drove to Downside and took him out for a pub lunch. Our favourite pub was in Priddy, a small Somerset village. The pub faces the village green on which a sheep fair is held in the spring and village cricket is played in the summer. It was an idyllic setting and we were always lucky enough to be there on a sunny day. We could eat and drink, and share our news while sitting at a table on the green. I lost a good and loyal friend when Father John died in his eightieth year on 1 February 2000.

As had become my habit, 9 August was regarded as a special day and was allocated to Edith Stein. After Mass I spent it quietly on my own at Combe Cottage and prayed and read as I reflected on the last six years. I was almost - but not quite - back where I started in 1984. I no longer had a pressing commitment to any one thing or person. My life could hardly be called 'aimless' but it ran according to my own timetable as in the past. There was more time for my family, especially my mother, as she grew older and more frail. Membership of the Secular Order ensured that my prayer life was regular and my friendship with Edith was as secure as ever. She remained my mainstay as I continued my busy, almost frenetic daily life.

In September - it is still 1990 - a friend, Stephanie Brooks, and I travelled to France to judge at the Connemara Pony Society show. We spent two busy days sorting the ponies, the good, the bad and the indifferent, before spending a day as tourists in the city of Tours. It was Sunday and I heard Mass in the resplendent Cathedral of St Martin - shades of Beuron and Edith - before exploring the city and boating down - or was it up? - the River Loire.

The Belgium Connemara Pony Society invited me to attend their show in October and I stayed with Eric and Beatrice Van Rijekevorsel in their gracious Belgian château that they shared with their two daughters and their son Constantine. A Catholic family, they had strong links with the Carmel of Kortrick where they took me for Sunday Mass. I felt very much at home with Eric and Beatrice and they were kind enough to provide a valuable 'stalk' in my daisy wreath in 1991. On my return to Birmingham Airport, I drove north and met Susan and Chris at Wood Hall. Dear Paddy continued to be our linchpin.

I took the final proofs of *Out of the Mist* to the printers on 20 November. It had kept me company on many lonely days and when the day came it was not easy to let the precious manuscript out of my hands. Another sense of loss was experienced as I did so. What a debt of gratitude I owed to Clare who gave me her unstinting help as I worked my way towards publication.

Christmas was spent with the family and the New Year (1991) in bed with the flu and a temperature. It took me some time to recover. My body finally said: enough is enough.

I collected *Out of the Mist* from the printers on 28 January and held a book launch in Hereford on 2 February. Many loyal Connemara friends travelled long distances to share the day with me. Jo, my Carmelite friends and my family assisted with the buffet lunch. It was a day of fulfilment and happiness. Coincidentally it was the sixty-ninth anniversary of Edith's confirmation in Speyer, the feast of the Presentation. This has long been one of my favourite feasts and it seemed that Our Lady and Edith might have arranged for me to 'turn the corner' on this special day.

On 24 February Jamie, a brother for Lara Lucy, was born, another welcome sign of new life.

My diary entry for 7 March reads: 'I unearthed all my Edith Stein literature today.' Yes, the time had come to resume reading and research into the life of Edith Stein. I was returning to Boars Hill for Easter and shortly afterwards planned a round-Britain trip to see how the Presteigne sisters had settled into their new Carmels. I was asked to prepare a talk and slide show on Edith's life, using slides and memories from my visits to Cologne, Dachau and Beuron. These I shared with each community at their recreation time. My journey took me northwards, first to Dumbarton in Scotland, from there to Wood Hall in Yorkshire, down the M62 and M6 to Liverpool and Preston, and finally due south down the M5 to Sclerder in Cornwall. The dual purpose of seeing old friends and sharing Edith with them more than repaid the many miles I had to travel.

I was happy to find that the sisters were, with great resolution, settling contentedly into their new environments. They were no longer the Presteigne sisters, 'my' sisters, but full members of their new communities. I felt a pang as I realized this. A direct result of these visits was a rekindling of my need to acquire a deeper understanding of Edith's life and works. This need was prompted by the various questions the sisters posed at the conclusion of my presentation. I was conscious of the many gaps in my study and was resolved to fill them. In due course, my quest became easier as further translations of Edith's spiritual writings were published.

On my return, I settled to reading a book I bought at Easter, *Edith Stein: Philosopher and Mystic* by Josephine Koeppel, OCD. It was Volume 12 in a series, *The Way of the Christian Mystics,* published by The Liturgical Press in the USA (1990). It has long since been out of print and I value my copy. Only as I opened its pages did I realize how hungry I was for further Edith reading. This book fed my appetite in a wholesome way.

Edith Stein: Philosopher and Mystic is written from the perspective of one who translated Edith's autobiography and who is also a Carmelite nun. For this reason I believe her observations and conclusions are more perceptive than most. On the opening page Koeppel writes: 'The story of an unforgettable person is given significant importance by the setting in which it is told. When an initial encounter is accompanied by an intense experience of wonder, . . . the groundwork is laid for a memorial in the heart. Giving the reader the experience of "discovering" Edith Stein, gradually, as the Carmelites in America did in the late 1940s, will lay a sound foundation for such a memorial.' Now, in 2003, I am sharing my ongoing 'discovery' of Edith Stein, which I owe in large part, not to Koeppel the author, but to Sister Josephine the person, a big 'daisy' in my wreath.

Sister Josephine places importance on Edith's fidelity to 'truth' from her earliest years and she writes, 'at every step along the way, Edith Stein was faithful to her lodestar of truth, and her code of personal conduct never changed.' She continues in this vein by casting a spotlight on the changes Göttingen and the war years wrought in Edith. 'Gone was her ready criticism, and in the remaining years it is easy to see how well she kept her vivid critical faculty under the control of a new, warm understanding of human nature.' Sister Josephine devotes an entire chapter to Edith's friendship with Hans Lipps, a friendship that is occasionally misinterpreted or guessed at. She provides intimate insights into life in Carmel and draws our attention to some of the realities of that life. 'As one needs to repeat, frequently, admission to a religious group does not automatically change one's personal tastes and preferences. Nor can one always make the most perfect moves either in giving or receiving loving cooperation. Carmel is no more paradise regained than is any other human relationship.'

My appreciation of this book was deepened by the fact that, although Sister Josephine had undoubtedly come to know Edith well, she never 'presumed' on her behalf. It is always: 'might she have?' or 'did she?' Like many another she asks why Edith was so reticent about her prayer life and she writes: 'Can we ever speak of her "way"? She who in her lifetime walked on so many lovely paths in the mountains, often without a guide, was content to go her way to God without leaving a trail for others to follow readily. But we have dependable signs to show it to us, nevertheless. The example of one who lives an authentic prayer life is enough, for "by their fruits you will know them."' Sister Josephine successfully encapsulates in one hundred and seventy pages the life and person of Edith Stein.

Friends in Germany kindly sent me a copy of the publication: *Edith Stein: Ihr Leben in Dokumenten und Bildern* by Amata Neyer. The text is in German but it provides a feast of photographs and documents concerning Edith's life. An English translation, *Edith Stein: Her Life in Photos and Documents*, followed, but not until 1999. This translation was undertaken by Waltraut Stein, Ph.D., Edith's grand-niece, and published by ICS. I found Jean de Fabrégues' small book, *Edith Stein: Philosopher, Carmelite Nun, Holocaust Martyr*, a fascinating portrait. Originally written and published in French under the title *La Conversion d'Edith Stein*, it was translated into English by Donald M. Antoine and first published in 1965 by St Paul Books & Media. My Edith library was growing steadily and each volume added grist to my mill, a mill that was grinding away slowly but surely.

1991 heralded the fourth centenary of the death of St John of the Cross. The Carmelite Order decided to celebrate by hosting an International Conference in London, *John of the Cross: A Fresh Approach*. It was held at the Digby Stuart College, 23–26 August. Susan, Chris and I were three of the one hundred and thirty delegates who attended. It was a unique gathering of religious and laity and is an experience we are unlikely to forget. The first two conferences were given by Ronald Rolheiser, OMI during which he dispelled the myth that John was somehow inhuman and pathologically single-minded. He portrayed him as an extraordinary mystic whose true obsession was love. In his second presentation he encouraged us by saying that John's advice to those who are struggling in prayer is as relevant in the 1990s as it was in the 1590s.

Father Kevin Culligan, OCD (from the USA), Richard Copsey, O Carm, Ursula Fleming and our own Iain Matthew, OCD provided papers on different aspects of John's life and personality. If we did not understand or appreciate John of the Cross at the end of these three concentrated days, then we probably never will. For the three of us it was invigorating to be in the company of so many Carmelites. To share the liturgy and conversation with them was, in itself, a gift. As we drove out of London we felt we had 'come of age' as members of the Carmelite family.

After my visit to Cologne Carmel in 1987, Sister Amata had included me in her address book. I felt highly privileged and indeed my pulse quickened whenever an envelope arrived with the Edith-Stein-Archiv imprint (there is no 'e' in the German spelling of Archive) in the left-hand corner of the envelope. The excitement had to be contained because the news – which usually arrived near Christmas or the New Year – was in German. On my return from London I found the familiar grey envelope in my post and wondered what had prompted a letter out of season. I was able to make sufficient sense of the enclosure to realize the Cologne community were planning celebrations for Edith's one hundredth birthday on 12 October. It was some weeks before the idea of travelling to Cologne to participate in the celebration occurred to me. By then it was almost too late.

I am unsure where the sudden burst of inspiration came from but come it did and I determined to go and say 'thank you' to Edith for her friendship and to share her birthday with her. It was, after all, a very special occasion. I discovered it was not easy to arrange, as there was no possibility of flying to Cologne from Birmingham Airport. The travel agent advised me my best route would be to fly to Brussels and to catch a train from there. The airport and railway station were some distance apart. In spite of all my travelling I am not very brave abroad and I did not relish the idea of finding my way from one place to the other. This is where the Van Rijekevorsel 'stalk' came in. I rang Beatrice and she immediately offered to meet the plane and to put me on the train and to do so again on my return. I wrote to Cologne Carmel who said they would provide me with a bed for the night. Surely I was only dreaming? On my return I wrote a short memoir for *Mount Carmel* and it appeared in the 1992 spring edition. Fresh memories are always the clearest and so I include it here.

* * * * *

The train rumbled out of Brussels Station on its way through the dark Belgian countryside, across the German border and finally to Cologne. I sat with my back to the engine for the three-hour journey and pondered my reasons for being there. I was aware that something stronger than myself had prompted me to be in Cologne for the centenary of Edith Stein's birth.

Was it, I wondered, to cement the friendship I have had with Edith Stein for the last ten years? Was it to say thank you for the inspiration she and her life have been for me through the dark moments and the heartaches? Or was it simply to share my intentions and those of my friends with her, in her homeland, where she had realized her Carmelite vocation?

The train journey passed quickly. I did not read or consciously pray. Neither did I sleep, weary as I was. No, I began to turn the pages of a mental picture book which I have drawn of Edith Stein's life. The pictures did not present themselves in chronological order. It was inevitable that the pages fell open on the eve of her forty-second birthday, fifty-eight years ago to the day, surely one of the most poignant scenes in her life. She had planned to spend her last day at home with her mother in the synagogue to celebrate the Jewish feast of Atonement. The following day she left home for Cologne and Carmel. A grief-stricken parting for mother and daughter.

From there the pages rolled back to reveal the everyday joys and sorrows as Edith passed through school, college and university which were rich in study and in play, in friendships and in success. Throughout this time she carried with her an underlying ceaseless search for the truth, and this is not hidden in my pictures.

And then I saw her slim intent figure bent over the book she had chosen from a friend's library and which she read from cover to cover through the night - the autobiography of a Spanish mystic which finally turned the key in the soul of the German Jewess.

I first came to know Edith Stein through her poem 'Holy Night'. The poem tells of her sister Rosa's journey to Christ and her union with him on her reception into the Church. It was Christmas Eve 1936. The church was brightly decorated with flowers - Christmas stars - and Edith was there to share the occasion with Rosa. She wrote:

> My Lord and God,
> You have guided me on a long dark road
> Stony and hard . . .
> a star rose before me gentle and clear,
> Steadily it guided me - and I followed
> . . .
> Now I possess you and will never leave you
> For wherever the road of life leads me you are beside me.

This provides me with one of the happier pictures in Edith's life.

I have visited Beuron Abbey and as I turned the next page I remembered sitting where Edith had so often prayed while on retreat or joining the Benedictine community for the Easter liturgy. Here it was that her spiritual journey was nourished and matured.

And finally two more goodbyes stare starkly from the pages of my picture book. Leaving her community in Cologne in 1939 and her adopted community in Echt, Holland, in 1942. These partings were filled with fortitude and pathos. 'Come,' she said to Rosa, 'let us go for our people.'

My train drew to a jerky halt and somewhat reluctantly I closed the pages of my book. Thirty minutes later I was standing on the doorstep of Cologne Carmel. It was 11.00 p.m.

I was welcomed by Sister Christina who spoke English. She led me up a climbing wooden spiral staircase to an attic room at the top of the house. She bade me goodnight and I was given a key for exit next day. I was secured under the roof of Cologne Carmel for one night. This was where I had felt called to be. I placed my picture book firmly under my pillow and fell asleep. It was twelve hours since I had left home.

The following day I shared breakfast and lunch with Father John Sullivan, OCD, who had travelled from Rome on a pilgrimage similar to my own, and Father Ulrich Dobhan, Carmelite Provincial from Munich. They concelebrated Mass with the Cardinal of Cologne and four secular priests.

The church bells rang out in a joyous peal of triumph and invitation. The seams of the church were soon stretched. A powerful mixed lay choir sang the Mass. The Carmelite sisters were in the church with the laity – there was no choir grille to divide us here. It is likely I was the only one present who did not speak German. I did not feel alone or apart. A strong sense of solidarity flowed through the celebration and the congregation. Edith Stein's icon, garlanded with flowers, was a sign of her presence among us, calling us to be one. The Fathers told me how the Cardinal spoke of Edith Stein's concept that no one lived for him/herself alone. In one of her treatises Edith wrote:

> This one for all and all for one is the essence of the Church.
>
> The more divine love fills the soul, the more the soul is capable of standing in for others . . . The divine can take the place of those nearest to him . . . and those he loves more effectively than others for one reason or another.

'*Ite, missa est*' concluded the Cardinal's Mass and he left the altar to share time with the community. The congregation dispersed gradually. Many paid a visit to the Edith Stein shrine in the crypt of the church, a symbolic, simple place of prayer. It is there I said my goodbye and thank you.

A prayer leaflet printed for the occasion contained Edith Stein's words, 'My longing for truth was nothing but prayer.' I hope my longing to share this occasion and the personal pilgrimage it became was also nothing but prayer.

* * * * *

When I came down from my 'eyrie' in the guest wing on 12 October I found I was sharing breakfast with an American. As he sat opposite me in an open-necked shirt there was nothing to indicate he was a Carmelite friar. Inevitably our conversation revolved around the day ahead and I discovered he was Father John Sullivan, OCD no less. I was, of course, aware that he was an editor at ICS (Institute of Carmelite Studies), publishing and responsible for the Collected Works of Edith Stein currently available. He had a deep regard for her and had played an important role in the promotion of her cause for beatification. I was soon at ease in his company. We did, after all, share the same friend and the same reason for being in Cologne at this time. Inevitably Father John provided another thread in my wreath and it was a great pleasure when our paths crossed again in 1996. By this time he was a Definitor of the Carmelite Order with special responsibility for the Secular Order.

On my return train journey to Brussels I had plenty to occupy my mind. The celebration Mass had been solemn and dignified as one might expect. It was the celebration of a life that had been cut short, but one that Carmelites and many others were beginning to value more and more. As I dozed I found myself opening a different book, the book of my own life. I turned the pages slowly. I was the child of a broken marriage, who went to a convent school as a boarder when war broke out, who learnt about God, the Catholic Church and right from wrong, during five happy years spent with the sisters. A new convert at the age of twenty-two, I was a lonely and shy Catholic who was encouraged by a good priest to join the Legion of Mary. Some years later I discovered Carmel and ultimately Edith Stein. On the other side of the coin, my life had been devoted to horses and ponies, never an easy way of earning a living. Only in my fifties had I discovered a love of the pen and of writing. Carmelites and Connemara ponies, unlikely companions as they surely are, came together to yield a life rich in variety and friendships. I thanked God for his many blessings but did not close the book. A few pages remain to be filled.

On my return to Brussels, Eric Van Rijekevorsel met me at the station and I was welcomed into the warmth of the family home. Emotionally, I felt totally spent but was able to share fragments of my experience with them and did the same at Kortrick Carmel after Mass the following morning. After a tour of Eric's Connemara ponies I joined the family for a performance of Krones Circus. The contrast from what I had shared the day before was almost too great. However, it did recall a happy early childhood memory of visiting Bertram Mills Circus at Olympia, always a special Christmas treat. Yes, there were happy family memories before the war tore us all apart and it was good to remember them.

On 14 December, the feast of St John of the Cross, a celebration Mass was held in Westminster Cathedral to bring the year to a conclusion. Father John Sullivan was invited to provide the homily and he was well chosen. St John became Edith's spiritual master when she was asked to write a *Festschrift* to celebrate the fourth centenary of his birth on 24 June 1542. She was celebrating his birth and work and we, forty-nine years later, his life and death. Edith's work was written during her final months at Echt Carmel and is, of course, *The Science of the Cross*. Who better to pay tribute to St John than Father John, a disciple of Edith's who had, in the same year, been celebrating the centenary of her birth? 1991 was a significant year for the Carmelite Order and it is unlikely anyone appreciated it to a greater extent than myself. As it drew to a close I marvelled at the rich heritage our Carmelite saints have bequeathed us: St Teresa of Avila, St John of the Cross, St Thérèse of Lisieux, St Teresa of the Andes, Blessed Elizabeth of the Trinity and Blessed Edith Stein who was then soon to be 'St'. Three of them are already Doctors of the Church. Who is to say there won't be a fourth before long?

CHAPTER NINE

I Meet Sister Josephine

Life continued on its usual busy way. By now I realized that to share my love and knowledge of the Connemara pony, whenever and wherever asked, was the only way I knew of putting my life back together again. I, and my expertise – such as it was – were needed and I responded to the need, a need that was so much easier for me to fulfil than the one at Carmel had been. I did so, secure in my pledge as a secular Carmelite and with, I hoped, Edith's encouragement. She once wrote: '[The Lord] ... can give us in a single moment what we need.' Was it not HE who provided me with the opportunities to use the gifts I had, many of which had been placed to one side in 1984 in order to fulfil, what I then believed to be, a higher vocation?

During the course of 1992, I spent three weeks in New Zealand and one each in Finland and Holland as a guest of the relevant societies. I treasure memories of the hospitality and friendship I received during my travels. Added to this was the pleasure that a host of Connemara ponies gave me as I met them in their changed environments, to which they had adapted so well. Each visit taught me something new and at the same time I found myself gathering material for another book, *Reflections through the Mist*.

Early in the year I took delivery of a Samsung word processor. Clare had battled manfully with my illegible handwriting and it was time to make her task easier. I have to confess that I never mastered the complexities of this little machine. It was portable and had many virtues but for me it was never more than a typewriter used with one finger. Writing had become compulsive, almost an addiction. I was more critical of my work and anxious to improve as I shared my memories of the people, the ponies and the places I had been privileged to meet, to know and to visit.

By now we had a new parish priest who decided he should live beside his church and return to Presteigne from Knighton. He oversaw the refurbishment of the original extern quarters, my former home, and subsequently Ty Mair became the priest's house. I was overjoyed and remained at Combe Cottage for the Easter celebrations for the first time since the sisters left. On Maundy Thursday I was commissioned as a minister of the Eucharist. This was a very special privilege, which I continue to value year on year. In September, I was one of three parish delegates to attend a Diocesan Liturgical Conference in Lampeter. It was an invigorating experience but parish circumstances were such that on our return we were unable to implement what we had learnt. I experienced frustration and a further disappointment.

In March I went to Oxford for the weekend with Rabbi Lionel Blue and Father Nicholas Madden, 'A Jewish Passover - Christian Eucharist'. I returned home with my cup full and with Volume 4 of The Collected Works of Edith Stein in my hand: *The Hidden Life*. The 'Essays, Meditations, and Spiritual Texts' are a moving collection of Edith's works written after she entered Carmel. This volume kept me closely involved with Edith for many weeks to come. Published in English in 1992, it had been available in German since 1987. *The Hidden Life* is edited by Dr Lucy Gelber - yet once again - this time in company with Michael Linssen, OCD. Waltraut Stein, Ph.D. undertook the translation and acknowledged the assistance she received from Edith's Carmelite friends, Sister Josephine and Fathers John Sullivan and Steven Payne.

In his 'Preface', Michael Linssen concludes with the following paragraph: 'In this volume the *Archivum Carmelitanum Edith Stein* wants not only to present to readers Edith Stein's conceptions of certain historical developments, graced persons, and a range of themes concerning the spiritual life, but also to facilitate a deeper look into the inner spiritual life of Edith Stein. And, last but not least, to also offer an orientation for one's own life in the following of Christ.' His words resonated as I developed my own thought and appreciation of this volume. I turned its pages slowly, imbibed the depth of Edith's faith and came to understand, more perfectly, her constant message of an acceptance of the Cross and of living in God's hands in our daily life.

I never fail to be impressed by the care and dedication that the editors and translators of Edith's work give to their task. Each article or manuscript in this volume is meticulously identified after careful research. Not every one is dated by Edith, but a letter or specific occasion fixes the date for the editors. Much of the work appears in print for the first time. A dialogue, *I Am Always in Your Midst*, is a poignant reminder of Edith's affectionate relationship with Mother Petra Brüning, one that I highlighted in *Edith Stein Discovered*. The original copy of the text is double-spaced and double-sided on six sheets, is folded in half, numbered and bound together with thread. I like to think this was written as a feast-day gift and presented with great care. It is a touching dialogue in which Edith expresses the anxieties she knew Mother Petra suffered for those in her care and gently provides some answers to the problems, saying during the course of the dialogue: 'One thing alone is certain: that God is and that his hand holds us in being.'

This miscellany of articles reveals the depths of Edith's relationship with God, if not how she achieved it or how she practised it. That remains her secret. Her message is clear for those who care to hear it, or to read it, in this singular collection of her writings.

On 5 July dear Flora passed into eternal life. By this time she was being cared for at Dysart Carmel and it was one step too far from Presteigne for me to attend her funeral. Vivien and many of her sisters from Dumbarton were able to do so and Vivien kindly wrote a moving account of the ceremony. On 15 November Monica joined her old friend Flora. I was pleased to be able to make the journey to Wood Hall to be with Paddy and her community for her funeral Mass and burial. These two gallant old sisters had lived their Carmelite vocation until the last chord. I respected and loved them for this and remembered fondly their place in my life.

On 15 October, three years to the day, Chris made her

Definitive Promise as a secular Carmelite. It was, of course, at Wood Hall and we thanked God for the blessings he had bestowed on her. The friendship that she, Susan and I had shared under Our Lady's patronage these past years, together with the benefit of Paddy's spiritual guidance and the welcome from Wood Hall, had finally seen the three of us safely into the family of Carmel.

During the year, my pony family had increased by one. In May, Chiltern Sunday produced her first foal, a colt, Chiltern Camogie. In July we – Jo and I – took them to the Breed Show where Sunday won her class and Camogie came second. We were justifiably proud of them both. Yet once again I was playing an active part in the life of the Connemara Society and was chairman of a committee that arranged for the selection and probation of young judges.

Lara Lucy was four years old and it gave me great pleasure to take her to a weekly 'Tots' Sunday school service held on a Thursday in their local parish church. I finally persuaded my mother to accept a 'home help' one day a week. Independent, as she always was, this was quite an achievement.

1992 became 1993, and in February I flew to Dublin with Kevin and Jane, Rosalie's brother and sister-in-law, to be with her for the celebration of her Silver Jubilee. An old friend of Rosalie's, Father Peter Fell, OSB, was chief celebrant at Mass with Abbot John and others concelebrating with him. The sisters arranged lunch at The Grand Hotel in Malahide for Rosalie's family and friends. We returned to Carmel for tea and further celebrations. It was a happy time for us all.

How was it that only now did I begin to ask myself questions? Why on earth were we celebrating this occasion in Dublin and not in Presteigne? Why had Presteigne Carmel closed? Why had it been a piecemeal operation and taken so long? Why had I been part of this prolonged closure and never questioned it or anything else for that matter? It was not my business and yet I was part of it. Why did I never shed a tear or any emotion throughout the whole sorry saga?

I arrived at Boars Hill in April for a weekend retreat with all these questions swirling around in my head. I was about to grieve in a way I had been unable to do earlier and was so grateful there was an Edith friend on hand to help me. Father John Hughes listened patiently to my disjointed story of events and my present anguish. His good advice, to stop mental wool-gathering with its whys, wherefores and what ifs, assisted me through this unexpected crisis. Not content with words, Father John offered me further comfort with a present, a poster he had just received from Rome. It was a copy of a recent portrait of Edith painted by a sister from Reno Carmel. Edith is almost full length with arms raised and with Rosa looking over her shoulder. And behind them a crowd of people with Auschwitz in the far distance. It is colourful, vibrant and telling, with the Jewish star attached to Edith's habit and with small children at her feet.

Rosa is so often the forgotten one but this portrait reminds us that she shared the journey to Auschwitz, as did the many more in this moving scene. The original painting hangs on the refectory wall of The Generalate in Rome. And my poster is framed and hangs in my oratory behind the chair where I sit and pray. The Stein sisters keep watch over me as I do so.

On 14 November my mother celebrated her ninetieth birthday. She did not want a big party and was happy to have her nearest family take her to lunch at the Radnorshire Arms in Presteigne. She remained able to live a remarkably active life.

It was six years since Sister Clare had left Presteigne. The necessary negotiations with Rome were finally completed, as was her trial period as a hermit. Bishop Mullins arranged to receive her and formally welcome her into the Diocese of Menevia in the parish church at Aberystwyth on 4 December. I was, of course, very happy to share the occasion with her. So many wheels had turned since that day in August 1988 when we moved her and her few belongings into Ael-y-Don. While some of the sisters experienced greater difficulty than others adapting to the necessary changes in their lives, Clare had been serene throughout and was visibly content.

Reflections through the Mist was ready for publication in February 1994. It had been a far less demanding task than the first two books. To relive my happy Connemara pony memories, to share my travels and friendships, was part and parcel of my healing process and put my life in perspective. *Reflections* was, all in all, a lighter read and likely, I thought, to appeal to a wider audience. In May, Jo and I filled the boot of the car with books and toured Ireland having pre-arranged meeting points in hotels and bars (the Irish equivalent of a pub) from Cork, to County Clare, to Connemara, to County Mayo, to Sligo and thence to Donegal. It was quite an adventure, but an 'instant' and satisfactory way of introducing the book to Ireland. We crossed the indescribably barren but beautiful landscape of The Burren for the first time; we visited the Yeats memorial in a Sligo churchyard; we stayed in simple homesteads and in stately mansions; we heard Mass in Ennis Cathedral and went to the picture house in the same town where we saw *Schindler's List*. We sold lots of books.

I mentioned earlier how in 1984 the younger of our two sheep dogs, Chloe, accompanied me to Presteigne. She adjusted to a much more sedentary life with a minimum of fuss. She continued to help me watch over the stock at morning and evening times, and accompanied me to the turn every time the bell rang for me. She slept by my bed at night and missed me whenever I was away. She was a constant, loyal companion. In August she endured two small strokes and I knew the time had come to say goodbye to her. It was an intensely painful parting and I found I was unable to replace her with another dog for two years. Combe Cottage was very empty without her.

I received an unexpected invitation to judge at Aachen in Germany, in September 1994. A group of young Connemara enthusiasts were organizing a show for their region and I was pleased to support their enterprise. Thanks to a friendly Carmelite 'mole', Sister Rosalie, any news concerning Edith Stein is passed onto me. Earlier in the year she mentioned that Sister Josephine Koeppel was spending twelve months at the Cologne Carmel in order to put the Edith Stein archives on computer for Sister Amata. I realized Aachen was not too far from Cologne and wondered if it would be possible to meet her during my stay in Germany. In reply to my letter to Sister Josephine, I received an enthusiastic welcome and my young pony friends were happy to drive me to and from Cologne. Yet once again Edith – yes, I am sure it was in her hands – provided the opportunity for me to meet another of her close friends.

Before we met, I built up a mental picture of Sister Josephine as a middle-aged, slim, scholarly American Carmelite. Instead I met a rotund, ageing but lively scholarly Carmelite who had a strong American accent but who was a native of Switzerland. It did not take long for us to feel at home in each other's company. I learnt how she had been taken to the USA by her family as a nine-year-old and that America had been her home ever since. German was her first language as a child and it was this that enabled her to work so closely with Edith's life and works. She did not enter Carmel until her late twenties and is a member of the Elysburg community in Pennsylvania. During the war a network of assistance was put in operation between American Carmelite sisters and their counterparts in Europe, many of whom were suffering grave hardship during and following the war. Care parcels were sent to Cologne where there was a special need when the community began the task of rebuilding their monastery. This is how Sister Josephine was introduced to Edith Stein.

In the early autumn of 1950, Elysburg Carmel received a small tan booklet containing twenty-four pages of German text. Its title, in red ink, identified the essay as *Das Weihnachtsgeheimnis* (*The Mystery of Christmas*). In small print was the author's name, Sr Teresia Benedicta, Edith Stein. The Cologne prioress, presumably Sister Renata Posselt, requested a translation. Two years later Sister Renata's biography of Edith arrived and sections of the book were translated and shared with the community at recreation during the winter months. It is likely that Sister Josephine had little idea how closely involved she would become with Edith Stein having undertaken these early translations.

Sister Josephine and I met in the Cologne parlour and were immediately at one. She would readily agree that it was she who did most of the talking, while I was an eager listener. I had been invited to stay for two nights and I soon discovered that Sister Josephine had laid careful plans for the following day. I knew from well-lived experience how Carmelite sisters are very good at this! She needed to visit Cologne city in order to extend her visitor's visa and to buy a piece of luggage for her return journey to the USA. I would accompany her. A taxi was ordered to pick us up at half-past nine so that we could spend the day together in Cologne. Needless to say, I had no argument with this plan.

When we met outside Carmel the following morning, I discovered how short Sister Josephine was and how infirm.

She told me that walking presented a problem but this did not deter her from achieving her objectives for the day. She wore an over-large pair of black sunglasses, the wings of which were as black and heavy as the lenses. She had a walking stick in her right hand and linked her left through mine. We had to wait patiently in a long queue to get her visa franked but had no difficulty in finding a suitable piece of hand luggage. Our business done, we had lunch in the railway station buffet and all the time I learnt more about Edith – and Josephine.

Sister Josephine had set her heart on making a personal pilgrimage while she had the opportunity. It was to pay homage to Albert the Great and Duns Scotus by visiting their respective tombs. These were apart but within walking distance, and infirm or not we made it. We must have looked an incongruous pair as we trudged the streets of a sun-bathed Cologne. Albert the Great was a German Dominican and Duns Scotus a Scottish Franciscan. They both died in Cologne. Thomas Aquinas, whose work, *Disputed Questions on Truth*, was translated by Edith, was a disciple of St Albert. And Edith tells us in her 'Preface' to *Finite and Eternal Being* that she followed Plato, Augustine and Duns Scotus. Thus, these two great philosophers, both from the thirteenth century, had influenced Edith's thought and work to varying degrees and were the reason for our pilgrimage. We shared a short meditation beside each tomb and inevitably my thoughts strayed to Edith. Might she have made a similar pilgrimage on a visit to Cologne, I wondered?

We returned to Carmel by taxi, but the day was not yet over. I was taken into a large, more or less empty room adjacent to the church. The walls were adorned with hand-drawn pictures, illustrations or sketches. I am not certain how best to describe these unique drawings which were mapped out by the founding prioress, Mother Isabella, as a means of educating those sisters who were illiterate. The wall was dotted with small, circular rose windows letting in the light. This remarkable piece of history, together with the main structure of the church, survived major war damage and remains testimony to Mother Isabella's resourcefulness when the foundation was made from Belgium more than three hundred years earlier in 1643. To end what had been an unparalleled day of pleasure and opportunity, I was taken through the enclosure to the room that housed the Edith Stein Archive. Sister knew how much this would mean to me and had asked Sister Amata's permission. We paid our visit while the community were at Vespers. This was where so much of Edith's life was stored and treasured. I sat for a few moments, breathed deeply and said a prayer of gratitude for all the gifts of the day.

The following morning, before saying goodbye, Sister Josephine and I exchanged gifts. She had a copy of the recently published *Self-Portrait in Letters 1916–1942*, translated by her, Volume 5 in the ICS Collected Works of Edith Stein. Inside she wrote: 'When one is so immediately "good friends" as we are it's a real gift from the Lord through Edith. I'll not forget you or today. Love Sr Josephine OCD.' In return, I gave her a copy of *Reflections through the Mist*. Because she had confided to me that her reading for relaxation was none other than Dick Francis, the renowned retired national hunt jockey and now a novelist crime writer, I hoped my *Reflections* might not come amiss.

My young German friends collected me at the appointed time. They met Sister Josephine and no longer held a fear of Carmelite enclosure walls behind which, they confided, they had been fearful to leave me forty-eight hours earlier!

During our time together, I learnt how Sister Josephine had previously spent six months in Cologne Carmel in 1970 to brush up her German prior to further work of translation, specifically I imagine *Life in a Jewish Family*. She told me how her life in Carmel allowed her five hours a day with Edith. How she had met members of Edith's family, not least her niece, Susanne Batzdorff, and how she had been able to attend Edith's beatification. She had visited Le Pâquier Carmel in Switzerland to see their archive material concerning the possibility of Edith's transfer to them towards the end of her life. She had, she told me, nearly died of cold in the Swiss Carmel and curtailed her visit. She was planning a journey to the Ursuline Convent at Dorsten in order to meet Mother Petra Brüning's niece, before her return to the USA. Sister Josephine's zest for life and zest for Edith was a tonic from which I drank deeply for many weeks to come.

Self-Portrait in Letters 1916–1942 increased my awareness of Edith's capacity for friendship: her ability to find time for all who sought her advice; the wisdom in the advice she gave;

and her own dependence on her closest friends. In the 'Editor's Preface', Cardinal Newman is quoted as saying 'that a man's life lies in his letters ... for arriving at the inside of things, the publication of letters is the true method.' The fact that so many of Edith's letters have survived indicates how greatly they were valued and treasured by those who received them. How grateful we – her latter-day friends – should be for this. I found Volume 5 an invaluable companion to Volume 1, *Life in a Jewish Family* and for me, at least, they completed her autobiography.

The book contains three hundred and forty-two letters. The first, dated 16 August 1916 from Breslau, is to a close friend from her days at university, Fritz Kaufmann. And the last, to her prioress in Echt Carmel dated 6 August 1942, is from the camp at Westerbork. I so much enjoyed catching a glimpse of the gentler, softer Edith, which so often eludes us. While many letters begin and end quite formally, when writing to her sister Erna she concludes, 'Love and kisses' and sixteen years later as a Carmelite nun she writes, 'I trust you will not be cross with me if I now sign myself as my sisters here call me' and concludes: 'In heartfelt love, your sister Benedicta'.

When Edith first met Fritz Kaufmann at Göttingen she chided him for his somewhat pretentious airs and graces. At the conclusion of a long letter to him she writes, 'Farewell and do please write soon to your old "patroness",' and below her signature: 'Incorrigible person!' In her letter she agrees that her friendship for Hans Lipps might be stronger than that of Fritz for Lipps. It is my belief that she rounds off this letter in a light-hearted fashion, to ensure their relationship is not impaired by this honest admission.

Edith's patient support for friends, who apparently came to rely upon it, is endless. I notice thirteen letters to a former student, Anneliese, in one of which she writes, 'God leads each of us on an individual way; one reaches the goal more easily and more quickly than another. We can do very little ourselves, compared to what is done to us. But that little bit we must do.' What comfort and encouragement lies in those few words. When writing to her religious friends, in Speyer and elsewhere, the tone is one of 'being on the same level' and she often responds to a request for advice.

The letters I enjoy most are those to her dear friend Hatti

and to Mother Petra Brüning. Edith is totally at ease in their company and in their friendship. She expresses joy at hearing from them and the possibility of seeing them in person. In Hatti she has a friend in phenomenology and in Mother Petra one in Christ. She can be totally 'herself' with them both. Many of her letters to Mother Petra conclude with gratitude and we are aware how much this friendship meant to her.

In October I drove to Sclerder Carmel. Sister Joan had been asked to join the three sisters in the Johannesburg Carmel, and being an intensely loyal person she had agreed to do so. I was sad to see her uprooting herself yet again. Joan and I had always been good friends and I hoped it would ease the good-byes at Sclerder if I picked her up and drove her to Heathrow. The situation of the Carmels in South Africa had been and still were very unsettled. The news from there had played a part in my own crisis earlier in the year but the ramifications of its comings and goings do not belong in this book. Joan and I enjoyed the long drive together from Cornwall to London and shared a picnic on the way. Would the final chapter of Presteigne Carmel ever close, I wondered.

Towards the end of the month I joined a group at Boars Hill for the second of Father John Hughes' Edith retreats: 'Seeker of Love and Truth: The Journey of Edith Stein to Faith'. I was pleased to be able to tell Father John that I had regained peace of mind and how grateful I was to him and to Edith for their friendship.

A Chiltern-bred pony, Chiltern Royalty, qualified for the big end-of-year Mountain and Moorland pony championships held at Olympia just before Christmas. Jo and I went to London to support her and her young rider and spent three nights away. We went to the theatre and Christmas-shopped and cheered Royalty's award as Reserve Champion. We wanted to shout to the world: 'We bred that lovely pony!' In spite of one or two reverses, 1994 had been a bountiful year and one to cherish.

CHAPTER TEN

The OCDS

The TOS, the Third Order Secular, appeared to make a slow and hesitant start. The initial Rule of Life was issued in 1678 by the Prior General Emilio Jacomelli and was not translated into English until 1719. In 1883, a full one hundred and sixty years later, the Definitory General issued an 'Official Rule', which must have overtaken or replaced the first. In 1911 this was revised and was subsequently approved by Pope Benedict XV in 1921. At the same time, the first official manual was published and the text included the following: 'the purpose of this Rule is to honour God and his Blessed Mother and to serve the Church through an ascetical and prayerful life.' I am indebted to Monica B O'Neill's *Teresian Carmelite Laity in Ireland – A Study in Spirituality and History* (privately published, Dublin, 1997) for this background information.

During the eighteenth and nineteenth centuries, many of the Tertiaries – this was their title in those times – led a quasi-religious life, often wearing a habit and living a devout life of personal prayer. There were few groups or communities. Individual members were isolated and were left to interpret and live their commitments to the Third Order as they thought best. In the twentieth century, some of the elements of religious life adopted by members were dropped. But at the same time a greater dependency on the friars was apparent.

The 1911 Rule sufficed until five years after the completion of the Second Vatican Council (1962–1965) when a further revision was required in the light of the Council's recommendations on the role of the laity. A revised edition was issued in 1970 for a trial period and was formally adopted in 1979. TOS was replaced by the Secular Order of Discalced Carmelites, the OCDS. Members were no longer Third Order or Tertiaries but responsible lay members of the Carmelite Order.

O'Neill tells us: 'The teaching of Vatican II had a profound impact on Secular Orders. It resulted in a reappraisal of their place in the Church, their identity, their rules of life and the way they were organised. In the case of the Secular Order of the Teresian Carmel, the Rule of Life was re-written in the light of Vatican II and the new understanding of the Third Orders. It . . . is noteworthy for its effort to involve members in the organisation of the OCDS and for its genuine attempt to encourage a lay expression of Teresian spirituality.'

Monica O'Neill's study is in four parts and concentrates primarily on the development and life of the Order in Ireland. There are few records available of the same in England. However, I have a copy of the minutes on the occasion of the establishment of a new Congregation of the Third Secular Order – you will notice both 'Third' and 'Secular' are employed here – in Kensington on 15 January 1953. It was the first Congregation to be erected, and fifty-four professed Tertiaries and twelve novices were present. Father Provincial made the appointments because members were not yet fully acquainted with each other. It is interesting to note the following. A Mother Prioress was appointed, together with a sub-prioress who was also mistress of novices. There then followed the appointment of a 1st, 2nd and 3rd 'discreet', a treasurer, a secretary, a 1st and 2nd infirmarian and a sacristan. I found myself asking: what was a 'discreet' and how did the infirmarians discharge their duties? How strange and archaic these appointments may appear fifty years later. On 4 December 1960 The Birmingham Congregation of the Sacred Heart was canonically erected. On this occasion, it is said, a group of isolated Carmelite Tertiaries came together, seventeen sisters, two brothers and a novice. When Birmingham was first formed it was for women only. This was also the case in Kensington. As I write, there is a second Congregation for men only in Kensington. There is no longer a Congregation in Birmingham but new groups are forming in the region as I write.

In 1971, Father John Bernard Keegan succeeded Father Ronan Murphy as National Director. He undertook to provide a monthly letter for Secular Order members because, as he wrote, 'they were scattered throughout the country and many were unable to meet together, except for an annual retreat and it was a means of keeping in touch and of forming them in Carmelite spirituality.' Father John Bernard wrote his monthly letter until 1983. Secular Carmelites owe him a sincere debt of gratitude for this generous giving of his time and wisdom for twelve long years.

The new Rule was implemented slowly and with a certain reluctance by some members. I do not remember being given a copy of the Rule when I began my formation but a copy of the monthly newsletter was passed on to me. By this time it was written by Father Tadgh Tierney – our new National Director – on what appeared to be an ancient typewriter using a single A4 sheet and roneoed off (duplicated). The content concerned the writings or life of one of our Carmelite saints. And if there was room at the foot of the page, your name was added if you had made your First or Definitive Promise. There was rarely any news to include until the Crewe meeting was being prepared in 1983. At the time I was a very raw novice and hardly a suitable delegate for that meeting, but I filled in the application form and hoped for the best. My application was not rejected and the meeting proved a defining moment for me.

The retreat centre used for the gathering had only recently opened and was being directed by a handful of brothers to whom it was a new experience. We found ourselves sharing small dormitories with total strangers and were very cold at night with insufficient bedding. Remarkably, the discomfort appeared to bond us together in record time and we were soon one big happy family.

Father Tadgh convened the meeting to which he invited several of the friars. They, together with some of the more seasoned and mature seculars, had prepared papers on the various aspects of the new Rule and these were open for discussion. We learnt how some groups were more structured than others and how there was a need for a formation programme. I was unable to contribute but was greatly stimulated by the input of others and saw my future as a member of the Secular Order as a positive one.

Father David Adams had a particular interest in the Secular Order and as editor of the Carmelites' official journal, *Mount Carmel*, he dedicated the 1986 summer edition entirely to it. His editorial, or introduction, ran to nine pages in which he assessed the benefits of the Crewe meeting and the prospects for the future. He described Crewe as a 'coming of age' which 'has arisen out of the Church's deeper understanding of the vocation of the laity . . . it opened up a new horizon and a deeper appreciation of community and belonging . . . a family with a common inspiration and ideal.'

In an article by a secular member, Dr Peter Flowerdew, these comments were endorsed by the following: 'This experience [Crewe] changed my perception of the Secular Order from that of a collection of isolated groups to one of a spiritual body within the Church, but a body that did not seem to have achieved a proper consciousness of itself.' I am sure that this was true and indicated what a long way we had yet to travel.

In 1993, Father Tadgh was appointed to the Australian Province. Father Matt Blake was asked to replace him as National Director of the Secular Order. Another of those needs – which seem to crop up in my life from time to time – immediately presented itself to me. Surely it was time the seculars were responsible for producing their own newsletter? I wrote to Father Matt and offered to edit and provide a quarterly newsletter on behalf of members. He accepted my offer and I began the task of generating interest from among the various groups. In 1986 there were said to be approximately five hundred members, half of whom did not belong to a group. The number of 'isolated' members had been allowed to grow and grow. Groups were attached to each of the Carmelite priories and the Carmelite sisters provided focal points of interest, as of course had been my personal experience. A priest assistant provided spiritual guidance to the groups and the dependency on the friars continued.

Anything new is certain to take time and effort and the newsletter was no exception. At my request, Sister Clare wrote the title in her beautiful script and we made a copy of Our Lady from a sketch Mother Michael had drawn many years earlier. I decided on an A5 format and anything up to twenty-four pages which, as it turned out, was quite ambitious. Members were not used to putting pen to paper and some were not afraid to say they would prefer receiving a monthly one-page letter as before. Father Matt was very supportive and his contribution to the newsletter every quarter was valuable and appreciated. Father Livinus Donohoe gallantly undertook to explore each article of the Rule, and it took him eight years to complete his task. I knew I could depend on these two contributions quarter by quarter and they formed the building blocks of the first edition in September 1994 and, indeed, subsequent editions.

I believed it was important to encourage members to become involved, to take an interest and to share their news. How could our friendship and knowledge of each other progress unless we did? Each group had its own identity and we could, I was sure, benefit from a common sharing of our ideals. Slowly but surely I, as editor, made friends and uncovered relevant news from home and abroad. I like to think most readers appreciated the varied content. I felt very blessed when Carmelite sisters, from different communities, agreed to contribute. They are an important part of our Carmelite family and it was good for them to become more 'visible' to secular members in this way.

As has so often been the case, my Carmelite interests seemed destined to run in parallel lines with those of Connemara. Shortly after making the commitment to the newsletter, a dream I had held for some time was about to be realized, that of establishing a museum in the West of Ireland with the Connemara pony as the theme. This became a huge challenge and an absorbing project and for three years (1998–2000) required my presence in Ireland for six months of the year. It would have been easy to say I could no longer find time to edit the newsletter, but I could not abandon it so early in its infancy. It was important to me that it grew and survived. And so with God's help I kept faith with my undertaking in spite of the extra pressures on my time.

The idea of providing a permanent home for my archive collection of pony photographs and memorabilia had strengthened when, for sentimental reasons, I purchased Cregg Lassie's box cart and working harness. Lassie and her owner, Jim Walsh, were some of my earliest friends when I began research for *Shrouded in Mist*. It was their photograph I used on the dust jacket of the book. I realized that precious artefacts such as the cart and harness, once part and parcel of the everyday lives of the people of Connemara, were in danger of being lost forever. And so I purchased them. I very nearly bought a semi-derelict old school house, Derryneen, with the intention of moving to Ireland to implement my dream. It was a flight of fancy, but happily wisdom prevailed when I faced the facts: my resources were insufficient and, anyway, I was too old to take the risks involved.

The dream lay fallow until 1997 when I revisited Clifden for the pony show in August. A friend, who was aware of my aspirations, suggested I visit 'the stat' (the local petrol station) and have a word with John Sweeney. I walked up a flight of rickety stairs to meet the local entrepreneur who was sitting behind his desk in a small rustic office. I introduced myself as Pat Lyne and he looked at me as much as to say Pat who? I elaborated and told him I had written *Shrouded in Mist*. He immediately grasped my hand and we have been friends ever since.

John was in the process of restoring the old Clifden railway complex that had fallen into a state of neglect and decay since the closure of the Galway to Clifden railway line in 1935. He was building a new hotel, and a complex of small shop units to its rear, at the same time preserving and restoring three of the original buildings. Together they formed an attractive courtyard. The saved buildings were the water tower, the original station house and the engine shed. The latter was earmarked as a museum and this is where I came in. I told John of my ideas and he told me his. The local archaeologist and his wife were to undertake the planning and design of the interior of the museum but he was sure they would be pleased to allocate space for a pony display.

The birth pangs and development of the museum were a realization of my dream and have their own story to tell – but that is for another time. Sufficient it is to say that in 1998 I found myself responsible for the entire project rather than being a small part of it. It was a greater challenge than I had anticipated but one which I relished.

During my three summers of exile in Ireland, my post was redirected and I managed to bring the newsletter out on time each quarter. As I began to put it together for the eighth consecutive year, I realized I was becoming stale and short of new ideas. It was time to hand it over to someone younger than myself who had greater computer skills. I sought a replacement, and after nine months Pam Murray volunteered to take my place. I said many prayers of gratefulness when we met at Boars Hill for the change-over and realized that I could not be passing the newsletter into safer hands.

Shortly after his appointment, Father Matt formed a small advisory committee to assist him in his new task of National Director. As editor I was invited to join six others. We each represented a different region and met at Boars Hill twice a year. These meetings were constructive and I am sure we all gained from the sharing that ensued. I hope Father Matt found us supportive and helpful as we assisted him in a variety of ways.

An International Conference for the Secular Order was arranged for October 1996 in Rome. This was an exciting new initiative. Two delegates from each country were invited to attend. The advisory council agreed that funds should be raised to subsidize the travelling expenses for one of them. I was chosen as that lucky one. Paul Worrallo, another member of the council, was prepared and able to pay his own fare and Father Matt would accompany us. I had not visited Rome before and was very uplifted at the prospect.

Father General Camilo Maccise was intent on a review of the life of the Secular Order and of the members' status within the Teresian family. Father John Sullivan, now one of the Definitors of the Order, was asked to prepare and to preside over the conference. It was a bonus for me to find an 'Edith companion' in the chair. Having shared breakfast with Father John in Cologne five years earlier, I considered him to be a friend. Before leaving England we received details of the programme and a daily timetable. I was filled with enthusiasm and hoped that I could make a positive contribution and bring home the fruits of the conference to share with others.

Matt had booked us in at the Villa Bassi, which was within easy walking distance of the Teresianum. We had to find our meals elsewhere and from the word go I experienced difficulties with the Italian cuisine. If you do not like pasta, ravioli and similar, there is little choice. Matt and Paul had to be very patient with me.

Father John opened the conference with a stirring call to

arms. It was, he told us, time to learn new things based on current trends. We needed to grow in our awareness of the Order and to act as 'secret agents'. The Order's expectations of us were high. Plenary sessions were arranged and we learnt to which working group we had been allocated. Each group studied a different topic: formation, the Rule, and the apostolate. I was pleased to be one of those studying the last one.

On day two, we gathered at nine o'clock and met Father General who was there to open the congress himself. His message echoed Father John's when he stressed the importance of our vocation as lay Carmelites, asking us to witness to the presence of God in the world. Prayer must be an attitude of life and we should aim to establish 'small schools of Christ' using Mary as our model. We were not religious *in* the world but lay people *living* in the world. It was important to open ourselves to the needs of today and to allow the Spirit to talk in us. I feel sure his words encouraged us as he stressed that secular members were not *loosely attached* to the Order but *important members* of it. It was a time of renewal for us all.

The conference hall was well equipped with microphones and translators. The working party I joined got down to brass tacks very quickly with a good co-ordinator and secretary, both of whom were open to all suggestions. We were a mixed multi-national group that included Father Borg from Canada, Sue Jackson from Australia, together with delegates from India, Singapore, Malaysia, Holland and Ireland. Sue gained access to a computer in order to prepare our paper and later she presented it with great resolve. I found it a privilege and an education to work with such a dedicated group.

It was a special joy and an additional bonus for me to discover a gallery adjacent to the conference hall in which were displayed montage panels presenting a pictorial overview of Edith Stein's life. As one might expect, any spare moments I had were spent there. Two photographs I had not seen before gave me further insights into a youthful Rosa and Adolf Reinach's widow, Anna. The text was as comprehensive as possible in such a presentation and I sensed it was Father John's project. We were in Rome for the one hundred and fifth anniversary of Edith's birth. I well realized that Father John could not let the occasion pass without celebrating. In addition, as a parting gift, all delegates received a commemorative envelope featuring an Edith Stein stamp franked by the Vatican and carrying the seal of the OCDS International Conference. What an unexpected treasure for my scrapbook.

The OCDS Congress commemorative envelope, 1996.

There was little opportunity for a private talk with Father John. When we did come together he told me he was engaged in some serious study of Edith's spiritual writings, and he realized it was an ongoing work in which he was happy to be employed. He handed me a copy of an article he had just completed, *Insights into the New Evangelization from Edith Stein*. In this paper he uses the heading, 'Edith Stein Realist and Letter Writer' and then proceeds to dissect a few lines from a letter written by Edith to a Dominican sister in February 1928. In doing so he tells us that Edith rarely lost contact with the humbler realities of life, in spite of her own high intellect. Her advice to her friend was that we should not break our links with the world, even if thoughts of the Divine in the contemplative life are so admirable and desirable. She writes that we can find God in the world by bringing God to the world. Hence Father John's premise that Edith has a message for secular Carmelites on the New Evangelisation, the theme of our present conference. Father John concluded his paper by asking us to share what God has given us and to let God guide the transmission.

As I read Father John's interpretation of these few lines written in a letter seventy years earlier, I was aware that I should spend more time with Edith's letters. There were many lessons to be learnt by careful reading. When I asked him for news of Edith's canonization I was told the Holy Father would have been happy, had it been possible, to arrange this at the time of the Eucharistic Congress in Poland in 1997 but - an authentic miracle was still awaited.

On what was supposed to be our final day in Rome, we crossed the city by means of three different buses in order to meet at the Generalate where the conference drew to a conclusion. We were given the opportunity to tour the Generalate. It is here that the main business of the Order is conducted. When we noticed one unoccupied room we rather cheekily suggested, to our guide, that it could be designated to the work of the Secular Order. When I returned to Rome two years later, this was a reality and I met Father Aloysius Deeney and his assistant working there. It was one of the many fruits of the first International Conference.

Father General concelebrated a sung Latin Mass, surrounded by his Carmelite brethren, in the beautiful basilica next door. Refreshments in the Generalate House were enjoyed amidst many sad goodbyes, at the end of an enriching six days. During his final words to us, Father Maccise called for a new dynamism for the apostolate of secular Carmelites and encouraged us 'to tune into Edith Stein'. I was already doing so and needed no further encouragement. To sum up our six days at the Conference, I include the reflections I wrote for the December 1996 edition of the OCDS newsletter:

> Safely home ... but only just! I found the Congress a demanding but very fruitful experience. Twenty countries were represented by two hundred delegates. Our common purpose to serve the Lord as secular Carmelites ensured there were no barriers, with the possible exception of language here and there.

Father John Sullivan presided over a caring and vocal assembly who readily exchanged their views and experiences, after having listened to the opening conferences with rapt attention.

Father Matt's intimate knowledge of Rome and its transport system ensured we were always in the right place at the right time. Paul's never-ending cheery sense of humour was very supportive. Time does not allow more than a reflection on a few of the highlights – with a promise of more to come in following newsletters.

A golden moment for me was Bishop Guy Gaucher's eloquent exposition on St Thérèse's childhood and family life. Another was the unexpected presence of Father General at our last full day, when the group secretaries were presenting the result of their working parties. Father had given us a challenging paper on the first day and I am sure he would agree the seculars' response was equally challenging.

12 October was the one hundred and fifth anniversary of Edith Stein's birth. We were all presented with a commemorative envelope carrying Edith's stamp and franked by the Vatican. This was very special for me.

One evening I found myself sitting beside Father General at an informal supper party at a local restaurant. On the same occasion Father Willie Moran entertained us with a splendid rendition of 'The Galway Shawl' which brought a whiff of the West of Ireland to the multi-national group sharing a meal in Rome.

The first Vespers of St Teresa were celebrated in the vast Teresianum chapel. The delegates were joined by all the friars and students of the house. Together we provided a choir worth recording for posterity.

The presence of the Holy Spirit in our working groups was tangible. I found the one in which I was working – sixteen delegates from ten nations – an enriching experience.

For one Old Age Pensioner at least the Congress had 'pilgrimage' overtones! I soon discovered that 'when in Rome' my conservative eating habits were a severe disadvantage. I found scrambling on and off lurching overfull buses (with or without baggage) a hazardous occupation. As was walking off the pavement in front of fast-moving vehicles and mopeds, traffic which never ceased day or night, accompanied by noisy horns and sirens. Trying to keep up with Matt's long strides between the Villa Bassi and the Teresianum morning and evening, and on two sightseeing tours, tested my stamina and my feet. The unreliable weather, violent thunderstorms and heavy rain interspersed by some glorious sunny days, tested my umbrella until it finally went on strike!

The grand finale was the celebration of St Teresa's feast in her own basilica the other side of the city and beside the Generalizia. We had to leave the Villa Bassi at 6.30 a.m. and travel on three different buses, arriving in time for a cappuccino and croissant before Mass. This was sung in Latin with Father General presiding and fifty Carmelite friars concelebrating. The basilica was packed and the celebration a fitting one. It was followed by a tour of the Generalizia offices and many fond farewells.

We three made for the airport with the news of a strike ringing in our ears. Too true, the Air Italia baggage handlers were on strike. There were no flights that day. The redoubtable Paul saved us an endless queue and transferred us to an early flight next morning. Back onto the train and into the city again and by now it was very wet. We were weary and it was a blessed relief to find beds for the night. As we hastened on our way I landed flat on my back, brolly and baggage flying. A spare piece of corrugated cardboard on the slippery pavement was the culprit. I was picked up by two handsome carabiniere, shaken and bruised but no bones broken. What an inglorious end to a glorious week.

During the months following the Congress, the stimulation it provided was, I hope, reflected in my daily life as a member of the Carmelite family. Happy memories and good intentions often bubbled to the surface. I trust my subsequent contributions to the newsletter passed on some of my enthusiasm for the future to Secular members in the UK.

Lisieux was designated as host to the Order's General Chapter in 1997. Secular members were invited to attend as 'observers'. It was the first time such a privilege had been extended to them. Following the chapter, Father Aloysius

Deeney was appointed to the post of Prefect of the Secretariat of the Secular Order and Affiliated Institutes. In due time he and his assistant occupied the vacant office we had noticed in the Generalate in 1996. His primary task was to set up a commission to examine the Rule of Life. A small international group of seculars were invited to undertake this task with Father Deeney. In 2002 a proposed text of the new OCDS Constitutions was presented to members worldwide. We were asked to send our comments and suggestions for changes and/or improvements to Rome.

A second International Congress of the Secular Order was held in Mexico in 2000. Judith Swarbrick from Preston bravely undertook the journey on her own and reported back to us. It appeared that the format was very similar to that of 1996. The central message was that there should be increased cooperation and co-responsibility on the part of seculars, both in group apostolates at home and in support of our OCDS brothers and sisters in mission countries. Father Maccise once again gave the Congress his time and full support and held a wide-ranging question-and-answer session with members.

Meanwhile, new shoots were beginning to show themselves in our region. Two members from a parish in Hereford expressed an interest in the Secular Order, as did a personal friend of mine. Susan was overwhelmed with work as a partner in her local practice and could rarely join us. Chris and I met with Eddie, Judy and Janet in Eddie's house once a month in the evening. Eddie produced a candle and a statue of Our Lady but it was not easy to be prayerful in his kitchen with the washing machine going and his boys passing through to grab an ice cream from the fridge every so often! We persevered and after eighteen months, on 11 November 1996, Father Matt came to Presteigne to receive the three new members for formation. We chose Presteigne for the reception, having no spiritual base in Hereford, and we invited Sister Clare to join us from Aberystwyth. Thus the old and the new came together. I prayed it might be a sign of 'new life after death', and that the laity, the secular Carmelites, could in a small way take over where the Religious had left off.

In the event Eddie did not persevere, finding his vocation elsewhere. And Judy died very unexpectedly and tragically, all too early in life. But this did not signal the end of our new shoots and others joined us in ones and twos. We no longer had Eddie's kitchen! And yet we needed to remain in the more central position of Hereford. The Poor Clare community had recently moved a few miles outside the city where they now had a purpose-built monastery with guest/retreat wing attached. It eventually became the regular meeting place of the Hereford Secular Community of Our Lady of Hope and Saint Thérèse.

I cannot record every unsolicited gift I receive from Edith Stein at regular intervals, but one of them should not pass unnoticed, a small slim booklet, four inches by six inches in a blue card cover with the following title: *A Celebration and Thanksgiving for EDITH STEIN* and inside: *Thoughts from her Writings with Meditative Responses from the New Testament Selected by PAUL T. COKE*, a private publication, printed by Hilleary & Petko, Monterey, in 1980.

Originally a gift from Paul T. Coke to a friend of mine, it is inscribed by him and dated: Austin, 28 April 1984. It was passed on to me on Edith's feast day, 9 August 1996. A short text is included at the end of the booklet and it suggests that Paul T. Coke was a member of the staff of the Episcopalian Theological Seminary in Austin, Texas, perhaps a minister or a professor. I treasure this simple but beautifully presented small booklet with its cream pages and the use of Eric Gill's Perpetua and Joanna typeface. Only one hundred copies were printed. The thoughtfully compiled text often keeps me company on special Edith days and I marvel how Edith and her message crossed more than one continent long before her beatification.

Secular Carmelites in the twenty-first century would do well to adopt Rosa Stein as their model. She lived in the shadow of her brilliant sister Edith, but in the last years of her life she shared her deep faith and her commitment to Carmel. It was Rosa's earnest wish to be accepted and clothed as an extern Carmelite sister of Echt Carmel. The community were unable to meet her request. And so, Rosa settled into the life of a secular Carmelite serving the community as best she could and praying alongside them. It was Edith who acted as her spiritual mentor when they met in the parlour for an hour each Sunday. Together the sisters' example and witness is an inspiration to us all.

CHAPTER ELEVEN

Canonization

The process from beatification towards canonization can appear to be long and tedious for those who wait expectantly. I was one of those on Edith Stein's behalf. At the same time, of course, I realized that beatification does not automatically lead to sainthood and that many of those who are beatified do not achieve it. Others, in the past, have taken a century or more to do so, but under Pope John Paul's wise stewardship a speedier process has been encouraged and so I, and many others, were full of hope that Edith would reach the altars of the Church sooner rather than later. Suggestions that a miracle ascribed to her intervention was being examined provided genuine expectations.

Some days remain forever fixed in one's memory, as if they had only happened yesterday. 17 May 1995 was such a day for me. Father Nicholas, had recently been appointed prior of Loughrea Priory County Galway and he promised to keep this day free for me. We lunched at a seafood restaurant and talked and talked before moving onto Coole Park, Gort, where we relived the literary days of Lady Gregory. We walked the spacious wooded gardens; we paused beside the lake – featured in the Yeats poem, 'The Wild Swans at Coole' – with not a swan in sight; we bemoaned the destruction of the old house, one so full of golden memories; we had a cup of tea in the converted stable block and shared our pleasure of reliving times past.

On our return to Loughrea, Nicholas took me on a guided

tour of St Brendan's Cathedral and the Carmelite Priory. Both enjoyed a wealth of history and this he shared with me. In the Priory church I was shown a window for which Nicholas had commissioned a stained glass design in honour of Edith Stein. I was so thrilled at the prospect of a dedication to Edith, in my very own backyard as it were, and I could not wait to see the real thing. Nicholas never fails to affirm my devotion to Edith and he suggested I visit the artist when I reached Dublin. His poor health brought his appointment as prior of Loughrea to a premature end. Nonetheless his time there was well spent, if only for the installation of the Edith window! I look on it as a memorial to his time in Loughrea as well as to Edith's life.

When I reached Dublin, I made contact with the artist, Phyllis Burke, and visited her on Sunday morning. The window was complete but in two halves. It could not be sealed together in her small studio. We shared a cup of coffee and talked endlessly about Edith. The photos I took that day reveal the vibrant colours of the window: blue, red, bronze and gold. I believe no postcard since has captured them so well. Here is Phyllis's description of her work: 'The window depicts the main stages of Edith Stein's life. The scroll at the bottom symbolizes her Jewish origins. We see a serious young student pondering on the questions of life - her particular interest in empathy - enveloped in the darkness of doubt and disbelief, emerging into the light of truth which she found in Christ, the personification of truth from whom Pilate is turning away. We see the Nazi persecution of the Jewish race and the evil that seems to overcome truth itself. Finally, we have the triumph of the Messiah.' The window was exhibited in the RHA Gallery in Dublin in July 1995 before being installed in the Priory church. It has become my personal place of pilgrimage. I never fail to visit Edith as I pass through Loughrea on my way to and from the far West of Ireland.

Thanks to my regular visits to Boars Hill, the opportunity to meet and foster my friendship with Joanne Mosley, who lives not far away, was greeted with enthusiasm. At this time Joanne was reaching the end of her thesis towards a doctorate. We greatly enjoyed sharing our love of Edith and our study of her life and work. New publications and information concerning Edith's progress to sainthood were, we found, never in short supply. There was always something fresh and new to debate. Joanne joined the Edith Stein Society of Germany and their newsletter invariably provoked interest and further dialogue. Joanne's fluent German and sharp intellect filled so many gaps for me. She was a great facilitator as I grappled with Edith's brilliant mind and philosophy from which my own limited mental resources were so far removed. The petals of this 'daisy', Joanne, opened wide and generously for me and together we came to know Edith better.

The tramlines of my life continued in tandem as I visited Sweden and Austria for the first time, and Finland for the second, on pony assignments. I spent many hours on the production of the OCDS newsletter. On periodic visits to Ireland, I collected further artefacts for the museum and brought them back to England for restoration; I was asked to write a short history of the life of the English Connemara Pony Society which celebrated fifty years in 1997; in November 1996 I was invited to give a talk to the Hereford Newman Circle on 'Edith Stein, Philosopher, Carmelite, Martyr'; I shared a set of slides on Edith's life with Carmelite communities and friends (the slides were a gift from my German friends, the Milleders); my own ponies continued to give me the greatest pleasure and an equal measure of success.

On a more sombre note, my mother went into a local retirement home for respite care following Christmas 1995 and after a few days there she asked if she could remain. It seemed a sensible idea but with hindsight I regret not encouraging her to return home and accept more help there. As it was, not long after settling in at West Eaton House, she had a fall and was in hospital for some days. A second fall some months later added to our concerns and her unhappiness. At her request we moved her to another home in Leominster where she stayed until she died in May 2000 in her ninety-seventh year. She remained alert mentally until the end but had long since lost any joy in life. Her expectations of the next life were minimal and I never cease to pray that when she arrived on the 'other side' she received a lovely surprise.

I found clearing my mother's flat, and ensuring she had what she required in the home, a very sad and stressful time. She had given my sister and myself so much and retained so little for herself, and it was never more apparent than at this moment. My usual robust health suffered and I found myself under the doctor and on medication. Dear Jo rented a cottage in Pembrokeshire for a week in September 1996 and our time there restored me before I had to leave for Rome and the conference.

In 1994, Templegate in the USA published *An Edith Stein Daybook: To Live at the Hand of the Lord*, translated by Susanne Batzdorff. The contents were selected from Edith's writings by Sister Amata who says in the preface: 'This book is intended to give the modern reader guidance and instruction year round through the words of Edith Stein ... Whoever delves into the pages of this book will be surprised at the wealth of ideas it offers for meditation.' I found that these short quotations provided a thought, a message, and a lesson, from which one can draw sustenance for the day ahead.

An interesting point of interest here is the translator, Susanne Batzdorff, a niece of Edith's and a daughter of her sister Erna. Earlier, in 1990, Templegate had published a selection of Edith's writings, *Edith Stein: Selected Writings.* These are prepared by Sister Amata from a German edition by Waltrand Herbstrith, 'With Comments, Reminiscences and Translations of her Prayers and Poems by her niece Susanne M. Batzdorff'. Also included is a translation of Edith's essay, 'How I Came to the Cologne Carmel', written on 18 December 1938. In two articles at the end of the book, one 'feels' Susanne's pain and her hurt at the distancing of Edith from her family that followed her conversion.

It seems to me that as the years have passed, Susanne comes closer to understanding her aunt, and the religion and life that she adopted at such great cost. Like her aunt Edith, Susanne is a stickler for the truth. In a dialogue with Dr Eugene Fisher on 'Edith Stein's Challenges for our Times' – reproduced in John Sullivan's compilation, *Holiness Befits Your House* – she writes: 'For me the path of my aunt Edith has actually provided a push toward more intensive involvement with Judaism. What she rejected, I felt impelled to learn more about, to delve into my Jewish heritage, to make it truly my own, so that I might say, with equal conviction, "This is the truth." I am not sure whether I shall ever get there. At this point I am prepared to admit that there are many truths. I am willing to grant that Edith Stein found hers elsewhere.'

Susanne tells us that her mother, Erna, maintained a vast correspondence with people all over the world, answering their many enquiries concerning Edith and her life. After her mother's death, Susanne found herself taking on the responsibilities and these have grown. Only recently a programme on Radio 3 featured Edith's life, to which Susanne made a substantial and moving contribution.

In 1998, Templegate published *Aunt Edith: The Jewish Heritage of a Catholic Saint* by Susanne M. Batzdorff. This book, written entirely by her, provides a delightful companion to Edith's autobiography and letters. Susanne's childhood memories of Breslau, her grandmother and other members of the Stein family are very pure and fresh. We get a taste of what it meant for the eldest and the youngest when Edith became a Catholic and left home. Many of the quotations pull at my heartstrings. Susanne's brother, Ernst Ludwig, when referring to his aunt in an essay writes: 'She brought something festive along on her visits, and in her presence, so it appeared, the everyday turned into a holiday mood. She radiated a cheerful serenity'; and then, after her conversion, 'This image . . . dissolved after the revelation of her conversion and her impending entry into a monastery . . . That was to us a dark, nocturnal aspect which no one understood and which she neither could nor would explain to anyone.' Hitherto, I had only joined in the suffering of Auguste and Edith, mother and daughter. Now I knew what it was like to be another member of Edith's family.

Susanne, in her writings about, and witness to, her aunt has done much to ease Jewish-Christian relations, which have been strained and often misunderstood. She, together with her mother Erna, her cousin Gerhard and his daughter Waltraut, have maintained their family links and their love and respect for aunt Edith. Waltraut Stein has trodden an equally valuable path in projecting Edith's works. Her grandfather Paul (Edith's eldest brother) and his wife Trude died in the concentration camp of Theresienstadt. His son, her father Gerhard, married a non-Jew, emigrated to the USA and followed his wife into the Protestant religion. Waltraut lives in Atlanta and is a Christian but not a Catholic. It was she who translated two volumes of Edith's works for the ICS as well as Amata Neyer's presentation of *Photos and Documents*, referred to earlier. She was present at Edith's beatification, and following this she joined a week-long pilgrimage sponsored by the Edith Stein Guild of New York City and led by Father John Sullivan. They visited a number of places important to Edith's spiritual life and she writes in the Atlanta Archdiocesan paper: 'We began to get a sense of how much this woman has already influenced the spirituality of German Catholics, and we were ourselves deeply moved by the evidence of her faith and steadfastness.'

In August 1995, the Trinity Media Trust in Enniskillen used the press to remind us that it was the fiftieth anniversary of the destruction of Hiroshima and Nagasaki by nuclear bomb. They were advocating prayers for peace and non-violence. Prayer cards and literature were available from them on request, to which I responded. I was overcome by an enclosure in the same envelope, an icon of Edith Stein, together with: *Some Guiding Reflections on the Icon of the Servant of Yahweh Blessed Teresia Benedicta of the Cross.* The design of the icon and the reflections were inspired by Father Emmanuel Charles McCarthy and dated 11 August 1992, Auschwitz. There was nothing to say who Father Emmanuel was or where he came from. I absorbed his moving reflections and include a short synopsis of them here.

As an introduction, Father Emmanuel tells us that an icon is an image of eternity touching time, an awareness of the 'Kingdom come' and the 'Kingdom coming'. We ponder it with a heart of faith and a spirit of gratitude for the workings of Divine Mercy upon us.

His reflections on the icon commence with the Day of Atonement, the holiest day in the Jewish year and Edith's date of birth. The ritual of this Holy Day requires the sacrifice of two goats, a bullock and a ram. This is the reason for their presence in the icon. The animals are sacrificed and the burnt offering is placed on a gold plate, the Mercy Seat, and offered to God. Edith stands on the gold plate. The goat on the right is not sacrificed. It is the scapegoat, laden with the sins of Israel and driven into the desert.

The railroad tracks going straight ahead lead to the black oven in Auschwitz, while those from right to left lead into a cloud, the cloud being a symbol of the presence of God. Note the skull on the oven, a symbol that was worn on the SS uniforms. Golgotha was the place of the skull, where atonement was made by Jesus for the sins of humanity. Auschwitz was Edith's Golgotha. Number 44074, on Edith's habit, was the number given to her in the Nazis' records. She holds the child Jesus in her left arm. He is dressed in striped pyjamas, the uniform of the prisoners in Auschwitz. The letters above the child's arm, 'IC' and 'XC', are the first and last letters of 'Jesus' and 'Christ' in Greek. The comb in Edith's right hand represents the care she gave to the children in the Westerbork camp.

The Christ Child sits on a book called 'Veritas', that is, truth. Edith's life commitment to truth is identified here. The scroll in the child's left hand reveals the words, 'This is my servant' in Hebrew. References to the Suffering Servant in the New Testament are numerous. Edith identified her life and destiny with Jesus, the Suffering Servant.

Father Emmanuel says in his conclusion: 'Blessed Teresia Benedicta of the Cross is the instrument of this God, made in His image, born into His Chosen People, baptised into His Chosen Servant.'

Father Emmanuel is nearly, but not quite, the last thread in my wreath. It was some time before I caught up with him on a more personal level. I was assisted in doing so by an article in the *St Anthony Messenger Magazine* (USA) written by John Bookser Feister, published in 1998. This article, like the icon, was one of my unexpected gifts from Edith. While sitting behind my desk in the museum I made an American friend, Kathleen Price. In the course of our exchange I discovered she shared my interest in Edith Stein. To encounter an Edith soulmate while sitting behind my desk in the Connemara pony museum in Clifden, County Galway was, at the very least, an unlikely event. Only Edith in her own mysterious and wonderful way could arrange such a happy chance. Kathleen and I came together for an evening meal on 9 August 2000 and celebrated Edith's feast day in conversation and friendship. She kindly gave me a copy of the *Messenger* article, aware that it would be of interest to me.

Three people were interviewed for the benefit of this carefully researched article. One of them was Father Emmanuel. I learnt that he was a Melkite Father, married with twelve children, the last of whom was born on 8 August 1984. She was named Teresia Benedicta. Father Emmanuel is a theologian and a co-founder of Pax Christi, USA and is known for his preaching on non-violence. He strongly believes there are no coincidences in life: 'God presents us with situations in which we freely choose.'

Certain dates hold a special significance for him, in particular the anniversary of the nuclear destruction of Hiroshima and Nagasaki on 6 and 9 August, 1945. In 1981, Father Emmanuel waited many months in Damascus for the arrival of the Melkite patriarch who was to ordain him. He was finally ordained to the diaconate on 6 August and to the priesthood on 9 August. He was drawn to Edith Stein when he learnt that she had died on one of his dates, 9 August. He undertook a study of her life and, like myself, read all he could find relating to it and came to regard her as 'like the incarnation of nonviolence'. That his twelfth child should be born on 8 August (sunrise 9 August at Auschwitz, he recalls) was surely no coincidence and she was named after Edith: Teresia Benedicta.

At two years of age, Benedicta helped herself to an overdose of Tylenol, without the knowledge of those caring for her, and as a result her liver was damaged beyond repair. The specialists gave her parents no hope of recovery. The family and friends placed Benedicta in Edith's care and prayed for healing through her intercession. Four days later, on 24 March 1987, it was recorded on her medical chart: 'This child has made a remarkable recovery.' The medical staff admitted they could in no way explain Benedicta's recovery and pronounced it a miracle. It was subsequently investigated by the officials in Rome and finally authenticated in 1997, ten years later. One of the doctors to testify to the commission Dr Kleinman, was as it so happened a Jew. Father Emmanuel was quoted in a newspaper as saying: 'our position is that this is not an accident, that it is purposeful and it is within the providence of God.' In Sister Josephine Koeppel's opinion, the healing of a child would have been very close to Edith's heart. What could be more fitting than the healing of one's own namesake?

As the possibility of Edith's canonization was being discussed among us at Boars Hill one day I remarked, 'I shall have to go to Rome for the ceremony'. Father Matt's immediate riposte was: 'Pat, on your return from the International Conference you vowed never to visit Rome again.' I was a little taken aback, remembering only too well that I had indeed said this. I replied: 'This is different. I *have* to go, Matt, but I could not manage it without you', never for a moment believing he would take me seriously – but he did. Just another little miracle along the way.

On 24 March, I received a fax from Father John Sullivan in Rome: 'In reply to yours, Edith Stein Miracle approved on 18 March by Congregation of Cardinals and Bishops. As of today we, too, await determination on time, place of rites. You're welcome.' It was a wonderful moment in time.

I felt moved to proclaim Edith's imminent canonization in the written word, by means of a personal portrait. She is so often characterized as an unsmiling academic and not as the approachable, compassionate, loyal friend that I had discovered her to be. Pen and paper and my trusty little 'Samsung' were thrust into action on 1 January 1998. It was my New Year's resolution. As I looked at the first blank sheet of paper, my courage failed me. Was I capable of writing about anything other than the Connemara pony, I asked myself? Encouragement came when I received an invitation to provide an appreciation of Edith Stein for *Carmelite Horizons*, a quarterly publication by the Anglo-Irish Province. This exciting undertaking very nearly ended in tears! I spent many hours preparing the article. Sister Clare typed it for me and it was despatched to Dublin. The editor sent it to Sister Rosalie asking her to curtail it by a given number of words. Rosalie has her own distinct style and when I read the proofs of the revised article, there it was, for all to see. The style of the article was no longer mine!

After a sleepless night, I rang the editor and suggested that I be allowed to do my own editing, to which he agreed. I was in Dublin at the time and spent an entire morning on the task. It proved a valuable learning curve and the article appeared in the 1998 summer edition. My morale rose a point or two when a request was received to include it in a similar publication in the USA.

When I returned to Ireland in April 1998, it was in anticipation of the opening of the museum on 1 May. Once it became apparent that this was very unlikely, I applied myself ever more diligently to my writing, sitting at a small wobbly table in a cottage at Ballinaboy, my West of Ireland base for the next five years. I was glad to have something positive to do while inwardly suffering endless frustration at the lack of progress on the museum. Edith and her life 'took over' and demanded all my attention.

Joanne was full of enthusiasm and encouragement for the project and offered to edit the text for me. Because our appreciation of Edith is mutual, I knew this would enhance my work and relieve the pressure on my poor punctuation and occasional slips. Just to encourage me still further, Joanne's mother offered to type the finished work. Surely Edith was behind this wonderful twinfold blessing?

I hurried home for five days in June in order to attend my friend Judy's funeral Mass. On my return to Clifden I discovered the entire future of the museum was in my hands. My work on *Edith Stein Discovered* was placed on one side until I returned to England in September. I had completed chapter five, the halfway point.

Father Matt made all the arrangements for our visit to Rome. We left Boars Hill early on Thursday 8 October and checked in at the Villa Bassi the same evening. The following morning we went by bus to the General House to collect our tickets for the canonization. Mine was number 304 in the Piazza del Sant'Uffizio, Braccio di Carlo Magno. I have it still.

The General House is a very homely place despite its preeminence. We were invited into the refectory for a cup of coffee and I sat opposite the painting of Edith and Rosa. At the same time I watched eighty-two-year-old Father Simeon peel an apple. Matt told me Father Simeon was Postulator General for the causes of saints and responsible for assembling the material and witnesses required. Edith's was the last cause in his care before retirement and provided him with a high note on which to relinquish his important work. I wanted to express my gratitude but he was Spanish and anyway too busy with his apple to listen to an excited incoherent Englishwoman. Instead I visited Father Deeney in the Secular Order Secretariat and we talked of the Order and the work he was doing on our behalf. For me this represented another mini-miracle; an aspiration inspired by the International Conference two years earlier had become a reality.

In the evening of the same day we walked to the Teresianum where Father John Sullivan delivered a lecture. It was a moving tribute to Edith who, he told us, never gave into parochialism. She was one who scrutinized the signs of the times and who can call us to account and challenge us. She was, he said, 'a pearl-seeker par excellence'. She read the Fathers of the Church and even undertook the translation of St John Chrysostom from the Greek, with some assistance. She was a woman of tenacity, devotion and honesty. The poster pictorial display of Edith's life was still in place and we took the opportunity to enjoy a further study of it.

On Saturday morning we made for St Peter's and watched the preparations for the big event the following day. Matt spotted Father Emmanuel McCarthy and I took a quick photograph. He had a lovely white beard and a kindly expression. He wore a black pill-box hat on his head, the usual headwear of a Melkite priest. Sadly, I could not identify Benedicta in his group. We saw Laura Meaux, who was privileged to be doing the English reading at Mass next day. Laura is an O Carm secular member, an American who lives in Germany, who had visited our Hereford group when in England some months earlier. We had a few words with her and it was all part of the build-up to the day ahead.

It was finally Sunday 11 October and the sun was shining in a clear blue sky. I met Matt in the hallway at 7.30 a.m. and we walked to the Piazza San Pietro a mere thirty minutes away. I believe I could have danced! We stopped on the way for a cappuccino and croissant and were in our seats by 8.15 a.m. We found the Irish contingent of Carmelite friars in the same block and to the side of us was a group from Echt, waving banners to ensure we knew who they were. The altar was bedecked in red, red roses and red gladioli. And Edith's portrait, in her Carmelite habit, hung over the entrance to St Peter's. There was row upon row of the scarlet and purple of the cardinals and bishops and a countless number of priests who concelebrated Mass with the Holy Father, including Father Emmanuel himself. I found the offertory procession very moving. Carmelite sisters, Dominican sisters and laity all had a part to play. One of them carried a large red book, which surely contained Edith's own spiritual writings. Benedicta received Holy Communion from the Pope himself and the rest of us remained where we were, as priests moved among us with ciboriums overflowing with hosts. The choir was vibrant and the day was timeless. My thoughts drifted to Breslau, Göttingen, Freiburg, Speyer, Beuron, Münster, Cologne, Echt, Westerbork and Auschwitz: Edith's journey in life, which had brought us to this great day.

We began to drift away from the Piazza about 12.30. Five hours had simply melted away. The anticipated meeting with the Pope and Edith's relatives had been cancelled on the grounds of the Pope's poor health. Even this disappointment could not detract from what we had experienced. Matt found a small restaurant where we shared a shrimp salad and a carafe of wine. We talked endlessly of the day's events and of all that Edith had bequeathed us and what it meant to us. The following day, the Carmelites planned various celebrations all of their own, in St Teresa's Basilica beside the Generalate. Matt and I joined them for an afternoon Mass in English at which Father Maccise concelebrated with his brethren. His short homily urged us, living in the age of communication as we do, to tune into the 'Edith Stein channel' – what a lovely thought! – and to learn her message of bearing the Cross in life, however it may present itself to each one of us. Father Sullivan led his one hundred and twenty American pilgrims in hymn-singing. There was an atmosphere of Carmelite joy and solidarity spilling across the aisles among the peoples of all nations who shared this final celebration.

I will never cease to be grateful to this, the last but one Carmelite friar in my wreath, Father Matt. He was the best of companions and without him it is certain that I would not have been in Rome for this special occasion. *Deo Gratias* for him and so many good and faithful Edith friends.

The flight home added a little spice of a different nature. Matt and I were seated on opposite sides of the plane. The lady beside me asked if she could move to my inside seat. She just *had* to be able to see the Alps as we flew over them, she told me. Esme Russell was eighty-two and in her youth had flown the De Havilland Gypsy Moth. Three months later, I watched her do so again – this time on television. The original wood and fabric biplane had acquired a windscreen for the programme, which was titled *Moth out of Mothballs* in *The Times* television choice. What a valiant old lady Esme was.

I returned home to work on *Edith Stein Discovered.* My task was more relevant than it had ever been. I regretted I had been blown off course by my involvement with the museum and had thus missed my target of completion by the end of Edith's canonization year. On 2 December, I delivered the first six chapters in draft form to Gracewing Publishing in Leominster. Four days later I was booked to give an Edith slide show and talk in the parish of Weobley. Very few people came, but among their number was a man I had not met before. It was none other than Tom Longford, the proprietor of Gracewing. When he introduced himself I noticed he had my chapters under his arm. He appreciated the Edith presentation and gave me encouragement. After Christmas I devoted all my time to writing.

On 15 December, I took possession of a puppy. A smallish black-and-tan bitch with white paws, collar and tip to her tail. I named her Hatti. Why? Because Hatti was Edith's best friend.

CHAPTER TWELVE

An Epilogue

I finally delivered the completed work, *Edith Stein Discovered: A Personal Portrait*, to Gracewing on 31 March 1999. It had been a supreme effort, a daily living with Edith. At times I was engulfed in her suffering and had difficulty expressing my concept of it. Empathy was Edith's touchstone but I do not believe sentimentality had any place in her disposition and I took care not to be drawn down this route. I posted a copy of my work to Father Nicholas who kindly agreed to write a foreword. There was still a long way to go before publication but now I could leave it in the capable hands of Jo Ashworth, editor at Gracewing. I returned to Ireland and my work in the museum.

I was invited to join and assist Father Matt who was giving a retreat in July: 'Truth and Love Need Each Other: Exploring the Life and Writings of St Edith Stein'. This was a privilege I could not miss, although it meant a long journey home in the middle of a busy season. We seemed to work well together. While Matt plumbed the depths of Edith's writings and spirituality, I sought to reveal the 'person', the very approachable human being whom I had come to value as a friend. I explored the rich diversity of her life in three stages and assured our listeners that Edith knew how to be happy as well as how to suffer. I shared some of the fruits of my own friendship with her. On the final evening, one of those attending the retreat joined me in a rendition of Edith's *Conversation at Night*, a dialogue between a prioress and Esther, written for Mother Antonia (prioress of Echt Carmel) for her birthday on 13 June 1941. It was a light-hearted performance of Edith's work but spoke to us, as Edith always does, of the importance of faithful prayer.

At the same time, one hundred miles away in Warwickshire, the Connemara Pony Society were holding their breed show, the climax of every pony breeder's year. It was the first time in thirty-five years that I had missed the event. What a strange irony that a Chiltern-bred pony should win the supreme championship and – I was not there to savour the success. Chiltern Quota was following in the footsteps of her grandmother, Arctic Moon, who had stood in the same hallowed position thirty years earlier. I was happy to be a proud breeder from a distance. To share my friendship with Edith at Boars Hill was, after all, of greater need at that moment in time.

On 1 October 1999 the Pope proclaimed Edith – now Saint Teresa Benedicta – Patroness of Europe in company with Saint Bridget of Sweden and Saint Catherine of Siena, an honour warmly welcomed by all who value Edith's place in the roll-call of the Church's saints. In the Pope's words: 'Today's proclamation of Edith Stein as a Co-Patroness of Europe is intended to raise on this Continent a banner of respect, tolerance and acceptance which invites all men and women to understand and appreciate each other, transcending their ethnic, cultural and religious differences in order to form a truly fraternal society.'

Edith Stein has caught the notice and imagination of many far beyond Europe's boundaries. Two new foundations of Carmelite sisters in Brazil and Uruguay have placed themselves under her patronage: colleges and schools often adopt her as their role-model: the O Carm Fathers, who work among the poorest people in Colombia, have placed themselves in her care, using her words: 'The star of Bethlehem remains a star in the dark night even today.'

The ICS celebrated Edith's canonization with the publication of Volume 7 of their Carmelite Studies: *Never Forget: Christian and Jewish Perspectives on Edith Stein.* Referred to as an anthology by Steven Payne, OCD, the ICS editor, it was published first in Germany by Plöger Verlag in 1990 and is the compilation of Waltraud Herbstrith, OCD with the English translation undertaken by Susanne Batzdorff. The ICS have included some additional articles in this publication that are of special interest to English-speaking readers. The book is an eclectic selection of articles and reminiscences from Jewish and Christian authors and former friends and acquaintances of Edith. It has joined my Edith Stein library and is valued for new and personal memories of her. In particular I appreciated a short biographical sketch by Daniel Feuling, OSB in which he writes: 'She united penetrating intellect and vivid feeling in an exceptional manner . . . She carried her knowledge and love from the shadow of the Old Testament to the light of the Gospel of Jesus and to the security of the church of Christ.'

In 1997, Sister Paddy made the difficult decision to transfer to a Carmel in Ireland. Her family, to whom she is very close, all live in the North of Ireland. Their journey to Wood Hall to visit her was a tedious, difficult one and as, inevitably, members of her family grew older it was unlikely to get any easier. Maybe, with the benefit of hindsight, it would have been wiser for Paddy to make the move to Ireland when Presteigne closed. Susan, Chris and I would certainly have been the poorer had she done so! Paddy has settled happily at Firhouse Carmel, Dublin where she has discovered a new skill, that of master printer. For the third time I found myself loading the boot of the car with Belmont print! On this occasion I transported it from Clare's flat in Aberystwyth to Firhouse Carmel. Needless to say, Paddy remains my good friend.

On 13 April 2000 Gracewing launched *Edith Stein Discovered* under the umbrella of the Presteigne Newman Circle. We met in the chapel annexe for a slide-show presentation of Edith Stein's life. Who would have thought I would one day stand in the sisters' choir – where I had so often craved to be able to join them in prayer – to introduce Edith Stein to a packed house! My niece Nicola and the children were there. As was my godson John and his brother Andrew who live in Devon, but happened to be working in Herefordshire; Stafford, a good friend, who lives in France but happened to be staying nearby; Father Matt who travelled all the way from Oxford; Fathers Bonaventure, Peter, Brian and Luke, and Brother Bernard (Belmont) and Father Michael (O Carm) who brought Sister Clare with him from Aberystwyth; together with Jo, members of the parish, and all my secular Carmelite friends. I could not have asked for more.

In August 2002, Kathleen Price attended the '60th Annual Memorial Mass' for Saint Edith Stein, celebrated on 17 August in The Lady Chapel of St Patrick's Cathedral, New York. She kindly remembered me and sent a copy of the programme, together with the suggestion that I might be interested in *A Retreat with Edith Stein: Trusting God's Purpose* by Patricia L Marks and published by St Anthony Messenger Press. The Edith Stein Guild provided me with Patricia's address and we exchanged our Edith publications. I found her retreat well worth following and I never cease to marvel at Edith's facility to act as a 'go-between'. Kathleen is in touch with me all too rarely, but Edith inspires her and this is evidence that our friendship endures.

12 October 2002 was a memorable day for members of the Hereford Secular Group. Father Matt visited us in order to confer Canonical Establishment on our group, Our Lady Queen of Hope and Saint Thérèse. No one can tell me it was a coincidence that this took place on Edith's birthday and in the former Carmelite chapel of Presteigne! Edith surely had a finger in the sequence of events.

The date was arranged in the first place to suit Father Matt's diary, and the venue was used as an alternative when we discovered that the Poor Clares' facility was already booked. I need hardly say what this day meant for me. All fifteen of us gathered to celebrate the occasion. And this included Susan, now retired, and able to join us regularly. Tony, Chris's husband, kindly came in order to play the organ, and elections took place. Chris and I agreed not to stand as candidates and thus a new council was elected to look after the future.

In May 2003 the General Definitory of the Carmelite Order, at their General Chapter in Avila, approved a text of Constitutions for the Secular Order for a five-year period *ad experimentum*. They take the place of the 1979 Rule and bring the Order in line with the friars and sisters who also live by a set of constitutions. Seculars are recognized as important and relevant members of the Carmelite family, such a different situation from when I became a member in 1980. The Constitutions tell us: 'The great Teresian Carmelite family is present in the world in many forms. The nucleus of this family is the Order of Discalced Carmelites – the friars, the enclosed nuns, the seculars. It is the one Order with the same charism.'

On 18 and 19 July 2003 I judged Connemara ponies for the last time, though I had hung up my 'travelling boots' four years earlier. Judging has always presented me with a challenge that I have relished. I shall miss it and all that goes with it. Chiltern Sunday has bred her last foal. I have had to accept I no longer have the strength to handle her offspring. A chapter in my life has closed but many happy memories remain.

Volume 6 of The Collected Works of Edith Stein – *The Science of the Cross*, translated by Josephine Koeppel – was published by the ICS in 2002 but did not reach England until 2003. It is a major work and not, as has sometimes been suggested, a lesser, incomplete one. Sister Josephine's customary dedication to detail and accuracy is apparent throughout and I ask myself: what is she working on now? We may be sure she is not idle and that Edith has another task ready for her.

I have had to limit the 'daisy wreath' to those I have met or with whom I have had some form of personal contact. There are many more who have stimulated my interest in Edith Stein and who should be part of an even larger wreath. I have already paid tribute to Renata Posselt, Waltraud Herbstrith, Susanne Batzdorff, Hilda Graef and Waltraut Stein. Two more must join them: Romaeus Leuven and Dr Lucy Gelber, who together did all the early work of bringing Edith's writings together. The many pages saved from destruction in the war required sorting and reconstruction. These were taken to the Husserl Archive in Leuven, Belgium, where Dr Gelber was working. In May 1955, the Edith Stein Archive was set up as the responsibility of the Dutch Province of the Discalced Carmelites. Father Romaeus was a Dutch Carmelite friar, and he and Dr Gelber worked together until 1982 by which time the Archive had moved to Brussels. Michael Linssen, OCD replaced Father Romaeus in 1982. Lucy Gelber died in June 2001 aged over ninety.

In 1999 Michael Linssen moved to Würzburg, Germany, taking with him the 'Archivum Carmelitanum Edith Stein', where he founded the 'International Edith Stein Institute of

Würzburg'. The primary work of the Institute is to prepare a complete edition of Edith's works (known, for short, as the ESGA), which will appear in twenty-five volumes published by Herder in Freiburg, Basle and Vienna. This was Michael Linssen's objective. He provides the final thread in my wreath and it is he who ties the knot.

My Carmelite 'mole' alerted me to the existence of the Würzburg Institute. I sent Father Michael a short email to tell him of my devotion to Edith Stein and to express an interest in his work. I asked if he had a copy of *Edith Stein Discovered* and sent him my best wishes. To my surprise and delight, his long email in reply provided a complete picture of his work at the Institute. At the same time he enquired how much was known of Edith Stein in England. He added: 'A copy of your book (if possible with dedication) would give me great pleasure.' I put a copy in the post without delay.

On 4 May 2001 I received the following email: 'Thank you very much for your beautiful "opus". Congratulations! It is an enrichment for the International Edith Stein Institute. With my best wishes to you for your work and your life. Fr Michael Linssen, OCD.' These few words were of greater significance and value to me than the handful of favourable press reviews that *Edith Stein Discovered* received. On 26 May I received an email from the Institute: 'It is very sad but it is not Father Michael answering you. Father Michael died on Wednesday.' He was only sixty-one. His death will be felt severely at the Institute and by his many friends. I was more sad than words can express and yet – we had never met.

On 15 February 2003 the letter that Edith Stein wrote to Pope Pius XI in April 1933 was released from the Vatican archives. One more piece of the jigsaw of Edith's life became public. I found it a very moving and respectful entreaty to the Pope for his understanding and acknowledgement of the oppression of the Jews, and indeed Catholics, in Germany. Edith foresaw that the situation could only get worse. She begins her letter: 'As a child of the Jewish people who, by the grace of God, for the past eleven years has also been a child of the Catholic Church, I dare to speak to the Father of Christendom . . .' To read this letter is to appreciate the depths of Edith's inner suffering on behalf of her people.

This story ends where it began, in the Presteigne cemetery.

The first occupants of the former monastery did not remain in residence for long. But long enough to obtain planning permission for four houses in the grounds surrounding the house. As a result, the cemetery became detached from the house and was no one's responsibility. The wooden crosses that marked the graves, which had hitherto been lovingly cleaned and varnished, broke and fell to the ground. The grass and the hedges grew and grew. The lack of care was heart-breaking. Eventually, the crosses were replaced by a simple pavement slab on which the identification of each sister has been attached. Today it is cared for in the summer months, when the grass is mown and the hedges are trimmed. It remains hidden and is a tranquil spot. I visit on special days in order to pray for, and with, my old friends.

The fields on which Sister Flora's cattle and my ponies once grazed are now covered with forty-four red-brick, box-like, semi-detached houses. Presteigne no longer has a resident priest and Knighton is no longer its twin parish. Presteigne is served from Hay-on-Wye, twenty miles away. We are very grateful to have Mass said in the church three mornings a week. It remains a treasured house of prayer. Today, the main house is occupied by Catholics, who act as caring stewards of the church. The small parish community count their blessings and happily share responsibility for the day-to-day running of God's house.

I have learnt to accept things as they are and not to grieve for the past. As I grow older, I realize I have something new to learn and that is: how to grow old gracefully; how to 'let go' of a busy life and how to appreciate time to read, time to work in the garden, time maybe to write some more, time to watch Lara ride her pony and Jamie play cricket, and above all time to pray more, and better. I do so – confident of Edith's continued friendship and watchful eye.

Bibliography

Works by Edith Stein

Life in a Jewish Family [1891–1916], tr. Josephine Koeppel, OCD, ICS Publications, Washington, DC, 1986.

Self-Portrait in Letters 1916–1942, tr. Josephine Koeppel, OCD, ICS Publications, Washington, DC, 1993.

The Hidden Life, tr. Waltraut Stein, ICS Publications, Washington, DC, 1992.

Essays on Woman, tr. Freda Mary Oben, ICS Publications, Washington, DC, 1996.

The Science of the Cross, tr. Josephine Koeppel, OCD, ICS Publications, Washington, DC, 2002.

The Prayer of the Church, tr. Darlington Carmel, 1987.

The Mystery of Christmas, tr. Josephine Rucker, SSJ, Darlington Carmel, 1985.

Selections of Writings by Edith Stein

An Edith Stein Daybook, ed. Amata Neyer, OCD, tr. Susanne M. Batzdorff, Templegate, Springfield, Illinois, 1994.

Edith Stein: Selected Writings, ed. Amata Neyer, OCD and Waltraud Herbstrith, OCD, tr. Susanne M. Batzdorff, Templegate, Springfield, Illinois, 1990.

Works on Edith Stein

Batzdorff, Susanne M., *Aunt Edith: The Jewish Heritage of a Catholic Saint*, Templegate, Springfield, Illinois, 1998.

Fabrégues, Jean de, *Edith Stein: Philosopher, Carmelite Nun,*

Holocaust Martyr, tr. Donald M. Antoine, St Paul Books & Media, Boston, Massachusetts, 1993.

Graef, Hilda C., *The Scholar and the Cross: The Life and Work of Edith Stein*, Longmans, Green & Co., London, 1955.

Herbstrith, Waltraud, OCD, *Edith Stein: A Biography*, tr. Bernard Bonowitz, OCSO, Harper & Row, San Francisco, 1985.

—— (ed.), *Never Forget: Christian and Jewish Perspectives on Edith Stein*, tr. Susanne M. Batzdorff, ICS Publications, Washington, DC, 1998.

Koeppel, Josephine, OCD, *Edith Stein: Philosopher and Mystic*, The Liturgical Press, Collegeville, Minnesota, 1990.

Lyne, Pat, OCDS, *Edith Stein Discovered: A Personal Portrait*, Gracewing, Leominster, 2000.

Marks, Patricia L., *A Retreat with Edith Stein: Trusting God's Purpose*, St Anthony Messenger Press, Cincinnati, Ohio, 2001.

Neyer, Amata, OCD, *Edith Stein: A Saint for our Times*, tr. Lucia Wiedenhöver, OCD, Darlington Carmel, 1975.

——, *Edith Stein: Ihr Leben in Dokumenten und Bildern*, Echter Verlag, Würzburg, 1987.

Oben, Freda Mary, *Edith Stein: Scholar, Feminist, Saint*, Alba House, New York, 1988.

——, *The Life and Thought of St. Edith Stein*, Alba House, New York, 2001.

[Posselt], Sister Teresia [Renata] de Spiritu Sancto, OCD, *Edith Stein*, trs. Cecily Hastings and Donald Nicholl, Sheed & Ward, London, 1952.

Sullivan, John, OCD (ed.), *Holiness Befits Your House: Canonization of Edith Stein – A Documentation*, ICS Publications, Washington, DC, 2000.

Articles reproduced from: *Mount Carmel*, Vol. 40, No. 1, Spring 1992.

OCDS newsletter, No. 10, December 1996.